Future of Business and Finance

The Future of Business and Finance book series features professional works aimed at defining, describing and charting the future trends in these fields. The focus is mainly on strategic directions, technological advances, and challenges and solutions which will affect the way we do business tomorrow. We also encourage books which focus on the future of sustainability and governance. Mainly written by practitioners, consultants and academic thinkers, the books are intended to spark and inform further discussions and developments.

More information about this series at http://www.springer.com/series/16360

Andreas Weber

# Digitalization for Value Creation

## Corporate Culture for a Digital World

Springer

Andreas Weber
Essen, Nordrhein-Westfalen, Germany

ISSN 2662-2467 ISSN 2662-2475 (electronic)
Future of Business and Finance
ISBN 978-3-030-36228-7 ISBN 978-3-030-36229-4 (eBook)
https://doi.org/10.1007/978-3-030-36229-4

Translation from the German language edition: Digitalisierung - Machen! Machen! Machen! by Andreas Weber. Copyright Springer Fachmedien Wiesbaden GmbH 2017. All Rights Reserved.



This Springer imprint is published by the registered company Springer Nature Switzerland AG.
The registered company address is: Gewerbestrasse 11, 6330 Cham, Switzerland

*For Miriam, my wife, my best friend and most loyal connection in life, both offline and online.*

# Foreword

Business models are going digital so quickly that no company can afford to ignore the transition. Clear differences emerge however, when it comes to who feels affected by digitalization in which way and how companies deal with it.

This business model digitalization is based on ever-increasing data gathering and processing, made possible by the automation of our processes and systems. Exponential growth is guaranteeing boosted performance while at the same time exerting downward pressure on the prices of the necessary hardware and software. The associated ongoing penetration of IT into all parts of life can be felt wherever prices for services or goods are falling to levels previously unknown or in the emergence of new conveniences or new-found time for doing what you love. Ever since the arrival of the smartphone, digitalization has become part of everyday life for individuals.

There is a risk with disruptive changes to business models that those swept up in the wave of digitalization might feel overwhelmed by it at the same time. Politicians of all stripes implore the need for action, but still we lack any concepts to implement. There is also a real need to implement these concepts quickly—an urgency that gives the old adage "the fast eat the slow" a whole new meaning. The selection ensuing from the speed of transformation will become the focus of our work and will have a considerable impact on how we do business in the manufacturing industry. But what does our digitalization strategy look like? This is the starting point of Andreas Weber's book.

He calls on us to move our focus away from products and toward value chains. It is a question of identifying your role in a value chain and working toward developing it but also safeguarding it. However necessary, there is no magic formula for implementation strategies; these should be adapted to fit the respective baseline situation. This requires appropriate management skills with a focus on staff and their creativity. The structures that once gave us security must be broken down and the focus changed to flexibility and adaptability. Cooperation between team members and enthusiastic management give organizations the confidence that they can overcome the challenges of digitalization. Once again, management finds itself in the role of enabler, even more so than before. In this culture, mistakes are not seen as obstacles, but rather as a driving force for progress.

The author encourages us ourselves to become the driving forces of disruptive change in our companies while at the same giving us pointers on how to succeed in this. We should use expertise and experience in our organizations not just to create sophisticated concepts but to start early with the implementation process. Experimentation goes hand in hand with learning here.

VDI Association of German Engineers, Jens Reichel
Chairman of Production and Logistics Division
Düsseldorf, Germany

# Preface

Digitalization is not an IT affair. Digitalization is the greatest change project that we have ever known. Data is circulating in unimaginable quantities and at unimaginable speed. We lack the imagination to grasp the true scale of it and when this exponential growth will ever slow down. Data is a source of global fascination, offering opportunity for companies across all sectors: data provides a new, subtle, and extraordinary way of observing customers and their actions. This is changing all value chains, whether we want it to or not, sucking us into the digital transformation at a relentless pace.

Digitalization is forcing a change in all of us. Nobody is immune to it. Both privately and professionally we have to find ways to move with the times. Resistance would be futile. So, hear my plea: train your adaptability; you and your team must embrace this constant state of change. As soon as you open up freedoms and thinking spaces, and discover how people can develop and blossom, then you have arrived at management 4.0. A positive attitude will help you discover how to expand your entrepreneurial synapses to a way of thinking that opens up a world of opportunities to you. I wish you all the very best!

Essen, Germany
Summer, 2019

Andreas Weber

# Acknowledgments

Adaptability involves gratitude too. Gratitude is a milestone where we can all delight in what we have achieved and where we can express the good feeling in words before moving onward.

I would like to take this opportunity to first thank my team. My team has had to learn how to deal with my "nutty" ideas and, in doing so, developed a real passion for the transformation process. The journey toward change is not easy for anyone, and that includes me. This has given me all the more respect for the willingness of each and every one to contribute to each phase.

I would like to thank my employer, Evonik Industries AG, for trustingly enabling me to hone my experience and knowledge of management tools for staff development, innovation, and digital transformation. The use of these tools is what leads to adaptability. Without these it would not have been possible to develop a model for changed value structures as a significant driving force behind digitalization.

I would also like to thank Gabriele Borgmann for her assistance during the writing process. Time and time again she has prompted me to develop a central theme and keep writing with her interesting questions, discussion, and phrasing.

I would also like to extend my thanks to the many experts in my network with whom I have been able to develop the topic of digitalization and adaptability in fascinating discussion, but also the skeptics who contributed to critical reflection.

And special thanks go to my wife, who has never failed to support me unreservedly on this journey. Thank you!

# Contents

# About the Author

**Andreas Weber MBA** studied electrical engineering with a major in electrical machinery at the Federal School of Electrical Engineering in Oldenburg. He graduated with a Master of Business Administration from the SMA Vienna where he wrote his doctoral thesis on "Problems and solutions in the outsourcing of industrial services." Over the past 25 years, he has held managerial and consultancy positions in the field of industrial and technical services in a variety of industrial companies in Europe, the NAFTA region, and the Middle East—including roles as a court-appointed expert for the civil courts of Düsseldorf and Cologne. In addition to this, he spent 15 years working as a freelance contractor for SMEs.

Prof. Dr. Andreas Weber has been the Vice President of Evonik Technology & Infrastructure since 2012. As the head of Customer Interface and Development within Technical Services, he holds responsibility for:

- Global business development
- The sales and marketing departments
- Innovation management
- Organizational development and strategy

Prof. Dr. Andreas Weber is also a sought-after keynote speaker and editor of several professional articles, including for *VDI news* and the magazine *Instandhaltung*.

He coauthored the ACATECH position paper "Smart Maintenance for Smart Factories" as well as the specialist article "Value-Chain-Service Zukunft der Instandhaltung" in the new edition of the book *Betriebliche Instandhaltung*. He is convinced that the future of industry and services depends on the success of a digital transformation process. In order to accelerate and simplify this process, he developed his "data-driven services" model, which he has successfully launched in a number of international companies. His aim is to expand on this model in a book for the manufacturing industry. He offers his model as a guide toward optimizing processes and effortlessly engineering change with the words of philosopher Confucius in mind: "He who knows the goal, can decide."

# List of Figures

# 1 Introduction: Waiting for Death?

Time marches on into the future. Never stopping, never slowing. It ticks at its own pace, dictating the earth's rotation and, with it, the gravitational force of the sun and moon. Time is a reliable phenomenon between the stars. Yet still, people all over the world have the feeling that time is racing ahead. But this is an illusion. Measuring equipment may have become more sophisticated, not to mention digital, since the invention of the sundial. Thinking spaces may be filling up with more information than ever before. Data volumes may be exploding and doubling almost every 2 years. But time has remained human to us, which is exactly what it always was on a personal level: an exhaustible resource that gives life a beginning and an end. In between lies an ocean full of possibilities. In the era of Industry 4.0, this ocean is made of data. Data is generated by sensors in machines, by using phones, e-mail programs, bank cards, by driving cars, shopping, surveillance cameras, electricity meters, GPS, with every click online. It flows through our lives in real time, measured in zettabytes, a unit which is difficult for the human brain to grasp given that 21 zeros follow each number. The vast ocean of data is set to reach roughly 40 zettabytes in a few years, "by the estimations of researchers this corresponds to 57 times the amount of sand grains on every beach on the earth" (Jüngling 2013). Mega has already been replaced with giga and tera. Soon we will learn to deal with peta, exa, zetta, and yotta too. Given that data is set to have the economic significance that energy once had, I am tempted to say that the industry's best times for boosted efficiency and success are yet to come.

Industry is in the midst of the next revolution. After hydro and steam power, mass production on electrically driven conveyor belts and IT-controlled production, industry has now arrived in the era of 4.0: the era of sophisticated digital architecture. Communications take place in real time, a remote-controlled exchange between man and machine and from machine to machine—the Internet of Things is here. Industry 4.0 is solutions oriented, and it is seeing cyber-physical systems assume a central role in business models for the first time. Amazon, HRS, Airbnb, and Uber do not produce any of the products, they offer themselves. They simply use algorithms to break down what customers are ordering and what producers have manufactured.

 
A. Weber, *Digitalization for Value Creation*, Future of Business and Finance,
https://doi.org/10.1007/978-3-030-36229-4_1

The business models of these companies consist of interpreting data and linking supply and demand in unprecedented ways. Companies anticipate what customers will want tomorrow and tap into the value chain stages of other companies in order to meet those demands. No one is getting in their way at the moment—people are simply watching with astonishment. This gives the impression that the German industry is delaying the Fourth Industrial Revolution, in spite of the fact that the risks posed to German companies by faster acting competitors are generally known. Why is data hoarded in silos instead of being linked up across companies? And why do we continue to wait for further disruptive attacks, instead of individually questioning and optimizing individual value chain stages, both retrospectively and prospectively?

As Vice President of an innovative industrial concern from Germany and a worldwide-leading specialty chemicals company, Evonik, I am responsible, amongst other things, for global business development and innovation management in technical services. Over the past few years I have dealt intensively with the Fourth Industrial Revolution in manufacturing, directing my attention to strategy and process optimization, full in the knowledge that what is regarded as innovative today may be obsolete tomorrow. The world is, after all, currently in the process of merging into one smart factory. No one can stop it, and no one can fully predict it. With this in mind, Germany's politicians should seek to broaden framework conditions so that companies might achieve worthwhile results. We have the state-of-the-art technology and IT solutions at our disposal to develop this architecture. The only thing that is missing is a simple, transparent, and quick-to-implement model. There is also a lack of enthusiasm for Industry 4.0 as a whole as well as a change in culture for handling mistakes. What is missing is a clear awareness that we are in the midst of the biggest change process that the manufacturing industry has ever experienced. Unfortunately, the manufacturing industry has trained its vision on shortcomings rather than potential, it is groaning under the impact of new challenges and failing to see the new opportunities emerging.

This realization motivated me to develop a model that I could establish beyond company borders: in partner and supplier companies as well as cross-sector companies in the production and services industry. This model, which I explain in this book for managers, service, maintenance, distribution and HR executives and project managers, is based on the following theory: Only by utilizing its data and technological potential can industry optimize value chain stages beyond company borders, only then can Industry 4.0 come alive and only then can we start to seize the opportunities of change. Here, it is not a question of using new systems and buying new machinery, but rather a modular approach, reconfiguring and upgrading production equipment and, ultimately, securing locations. With this in mind, Evonik is now using information from now redundant data silos, linking these up with additional data sources, facilitating a step-by-step modernization around the assets of the group.

This book is intended as a written and visual guide to this success model—a call to action—while at the same time a warning against the pitfalls of obsessing over the detail.

The German industry is destined for failure if it gets lost in the details before it has even started, sifting through its future strategy for every possible consequence. There is simply no time for that.

Implementing Industry 4.0 requires a fast pace, one much quicker than that of inventors and skeptics. It requires people with expertise and creative enthusiasm who work on the basis of the 30–70 rule. The 30–70 rule? That is 30% of time spent on preparation and 70% of time dedicated to the launch, implementation, monetization, the trial process, as well as learning and adapting to changing conditions. The contemplation of objectives should not dictate the process. Objectives should instead be transferred from paper to the heads of employees, there in the midbrain where they generate that special neural mix of endorphins that takes you beyond the usual routine. The words of Joseph von Eichendorff still ring true here: (loosely translated) "an enthusiast is always on top of the world."

This book is intended as a plea for enthusiasm in transformation. This is because I am convinced that organizations unwilling to change from the inside out on the basis of fear or economic considerations and which do not recognize the creative opportunities currently available to them, will be changed by others. This book is a call to arms for companies to recognize and counter this risk ahead of time. It also seeks to get to the bottom of some allegedly complex subject matters. It aims to show that transparency on the global net leaves no room for secrecy, that technologies are merging together, that digitalization is uniting this beautiful world—interwoven by one shared web of data. The manufacturing industry needs to recognize the value in these data cascades and develop them, gradually and enthusiastically.

As Confucius said, "only he who knows the goal, can decide." The path to digitalization is known, the destination not so much. Who knows, maybe in 20 years we will see computers with personalities or independent machine-to-machine communication. Maybe we will see the emergence of supercomputers with super brains and intelligence superior to that of humans or even the first expressions of emotion. We just do not know. But one thing is for sure: waiting for the future would be commercial suicide.

## Reference

Jüngling T (2013) Datenvolumen verdoppelt sich alle zwei Jahre. Die Welt. https://www.welt.de/wirtschaft/webwelt/article118099520/Datenvolumen-verdoppelt-sich-alle-zwei-Jahre.html. Accessed 21 July 2016

# 2 Data-Driven Services: Model for an Industrial Turning Point

Denial is pointless: Digitalization is coming at industry with full force. Everyone is affected, nobody can escape. Unseen by many business leaders, we are in the midst of a change that is questioning the tried and trusted so radically that an industrial turning point is inevitable. At the same time the consistent use of digital technologies is giving rise to new unimagined possibilities nobody could have dreamed of even just a few years ago. The time has come for industry to make the transition into digitized value chains. You have to be in it to win it. Those who delay, hesitate, or wait have already lost.

The seriousness of the current situation is illustrated with the help of an academic model. The data-driven services (DDS) model aims to explain the current transformation process to decision-makers and create an awareness for the urgency of the impending changes. This is an enormous and complex task. Change is taking place in so many different parts of the company at such a rate that trying to keep your bearings can feel dizzying. After a number of discussions, it has occurred to me that one of the greatest challenges lies in understanding the change process. Even in top-level executive discussions there is often the opinion that digitalization is nothing more than the next big trend—just like countless others that shake up the economy every now and then. Many company leaders' inactivity is based on the experience that trends are not necessarily better withstood as "first movers." But this time, they are wrong. Digitalization is not a trend. It is not the "next big thing." We are being changed by the technological possibilities of digitalization, and we are driven by global technological change.

Today, we as companies and people are capable of operating globally almost without restriction. We have everything we need for this: goods, products, services—even the necessary computing capacity is available. The data-driven services model demonstrates how digitalization is changing production chains as a result. It serves as a guiding framework that enables identified elements to be assigned to objectives and allows us to recognize that all measures function and constitute sub-steps which come together to produce the greater whole.



A. Weber, *Digitalization for Value Creation*, Future of Business and Finance,
https://doi.org/10.1007/978-3-030-36229-4_2

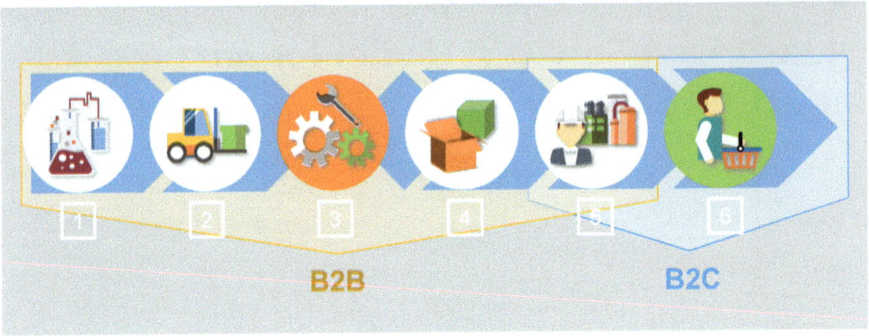


**Fig. 2.1** Supply chain diagram 1–6

In personal conversations the DDS model has always been in effective as a means of demonstrating to managers and entrepreneurs why it is necessary to understand changes. Using simple examples, I show which measures should be introduced and which tools can assist in this. With an accurate image of the changes in mind, the urgent need for action becomes clear—and comprehensible.

Dealing with the subject of data-driven services inevitably leads to the key question that everyone with ambitions in the industrial environment must ask themselves: What is my, our, the department's and the company's role in the value creation chain? How do I succeed in efficiently and flexibly responding to demand using concerted efforts? The data-driven services model starts with determining the supply chain. Changes to industry become apparent most quickly here.

**Supply Chain Diagram**

Traditionally, supply chains—shown here in simplified form—in industry have the same or a similar structure (see also Fig. 2.1):

1. Company buys commodity from upstream supplier.
2. Logistics delivers the commodity to plant.
3. Production stage.
4. Logistics delivers product to customers.
5. Further processing.
6. Marketing to end customers.

This is how classic value creation chains emerge. These will have to take on a digital character in the course of the transformation. Information is linked and supplied together with the products.

In the next step the supply chain model is expanded to include the machinery and elements necessary for the development and manufacture of the actual product. These are described in depth in DIN ISO 55000 in the context of plant and life cycle. Every company must broach the following issues:

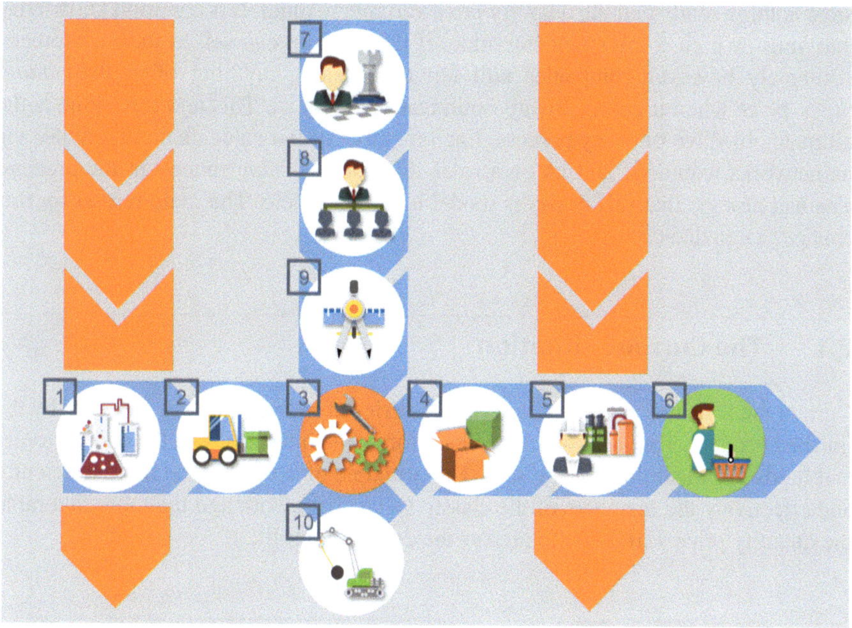


**Fig. 2.2** Supply chain with machinery and elements

7. Process technology—how should the product be manufactured?
8. Planning the production engineering system
9. Building the production engineering system
10. Production stage
11. Dismantling after use

A glance at the resulting diagram, shown in Fig. 2.2, illustrates that where continuous production processes take place along the supply chain, plant life cycles, and production stations run parallel to one another (shown vertically in the model). The result is an overall picture of linked system structures along the value chain. This supply chain overview complete with asset structures is necessary to gain an understanding that changes occur holistically.

Standard procedure is that each production plant is geared toward the product being marketed. Each company and staff member can develop their own concepts at the various stages along the value chain. The key determining factor in modern value chains is how a company can most effectively and most efficiently place their own product or service with the customer. The result is a wider picture of modern value chains with networked production flows, such as those used in the automotive industry segment.

These value chains function solely on the basis of the variables *quantity* × *price*. Here the sole focus is the respective next step in the value chain. Even marketing experts who involve the customer's customer in their considerations and planning have nothing more than the quantity price variable in mind. It is common knowledge that your own customers will buy more if they in turn can sell to their customers. Ultimately however companies still fail to consider anything other than *quantity* × *price* when it comes to any optimization attempts. This and this alone is the ultimate objective of every process. Each member of the value chain distributes via its networks, contacts, and its own sales division—earning money in the process. The bad news is that this business model is now obsolete. The main reason for this change? Digitalization.

## 2.1 The Current Situation

Current value chains are characterized by a series of individual steps followed by the finished product. The last link in the chain forms the interface with the end customer and holds responsibility for the sale. The principle of success? The more efficiently and effectively the members of the classic value chain work and the more favorable the quantity price variable, the greater the company profit.

## 2.2 The Future Situation

Progressive digitalization in all processes right up to the customer is triggering colossal changes in the value chain. While up until now production has always been the focus of interests, the customer has suddenly been pushed to the forefront, i.e., the customer is becoming a key factor in digitized value chains. All subsequent steps in the value chain will then be geared toward their benefit, experiences, and evaluations (see Fig. 2.3).

How is that supposed to work? This is the question you are probably about to ask. And quite rightly so. Customers are already clearly expressing their desires, requirements, and interest in products. To do so they use a variety of different channels, social media, for example. The primary task in business will soon be understanding customers. This will require a learning process, given the apparent lack of contact between product manufacturers and end customers in classic value chains. Where it was once the job of the marketing department to establish contact with the end customer, communication is now taking place over a variety of channels. And that is not all. Modern digital communication is taking place more intensively, more substantially, and often in real time. Added to this is the emotional level on which customers clearly express their desires, requirements, and opinions.

This is a dramatic change given that end customer communications were once the exclusive knowledge of the seller. Almost every consumer action leaves behind a data trail. A lot of data—and all of it valuable. The more data we have, the better we can get to know our customers. Generally speaking, digital communication can be divided into two broad categories—"active customer communication" and "passive customer communication" (see Fig. 2.4).

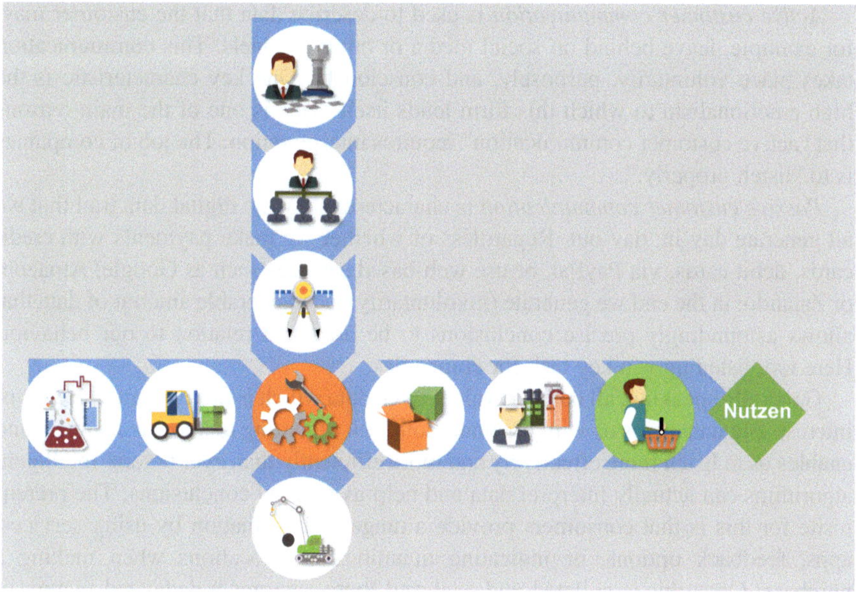


**Fig. 2.3** Supply chain with focus on customer benefit

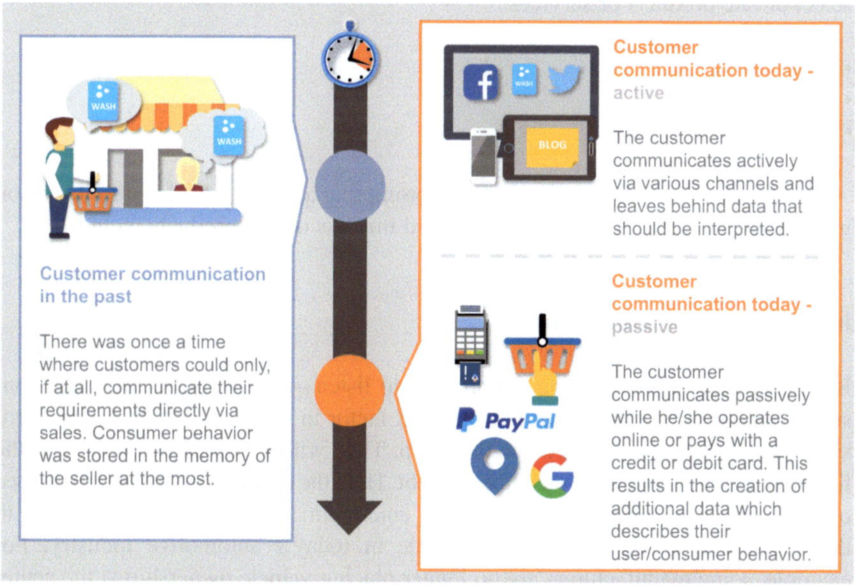


**Fig. 2.4** Customer communication

*Active customer communication* is used to describe data that the customer may, for example, leave behind on social media or other channels. This communication takes place voluntarily, purposely, and consciously. One key characteristic is the high emotionalism to which this form lends itself. This is one of the main reasons that "active customer communication" requires interpretation. The job of companies is to "listen properly."

*Passive customer communication* is characterized by the digital data trail that we all generate day-in, day-out. Regardless of whether we make payments with credit cards, debit cards, via PayPal, or use web-based services such as Google, Amazon, or Zalando: in the end we generate (involuntarily) a considerable amount of data that allows astoundingly precise conclusions to be drawn in relation to our behavior. Here too, listening is a key task for companies.

Generally speaking, all data has value. Even data which is not communicated is of interest. Big data helps us with the mammoth task of getting to know consumers and enables us to listen more effectively and more efficiently than ever before. Intelligent algorithms can actually interpret data and help us to draw conclusions. The prerequisite for this is that consumers provide a range of information by using services, apps, feedback options, or indicating quantities and locations when making a purchase. Once this is collated and analyzed there emerges a dedicated picture of real consumer demand.

According to my model there are three basic benchmarks by which consumers select or rate products or services:

- Fun
- Entertainment
- Value.

The insights provided by Big Data are prompting a need for backward integration with regard to value chains—the associated impacts on the products included.

## Impacts on the Value Chain

Big data offers companies the opportunity to listen—and to understand. The consumer benefit is becoming the all-important factor in value chains. In future retrospective value chains will become the norm. They will no longer center around the final product but around the customer benefit. Here the consumer benefit is measured on the basis of customer standards of fun, entertainment, and value. Approaches to this new development are already visible in today's automotive industry. For example, some manufacturers are no longer placing vehicle ownership at the center of their business operations, but developing entire mobility concepts in line with individual requirements.

This transformation is seeing changes on the vertical level of the model (see Fig. 2.5), i.e., process engineering, production facility planning and construction as well as the production phase and dismantling must be geared towards customer

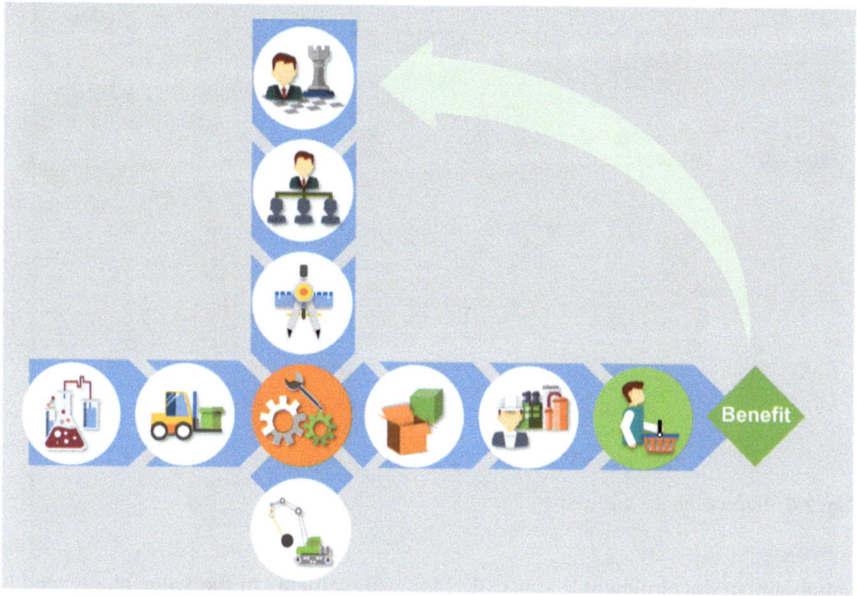


**Fig. 2.5** Customer benefit factor in value chain

benefit too. The ensuing structure must be flexible and responsive, after all: the constant acquisition of data from the ongoing consumer data flow can only be fully utilized for strategic purposes if the value chain can react quickly to the acquired findings.

Gearing the value chain toward customer benefit makes it even more volatile because not only do quantities, quality, and properties change but also the entire production process does andnd at immense speed. This requires the manufacture of the "right" product at the right time, in the right place and the right quantity: this confronts the manufacturer with the virtually impossible task of reserving the necessary plant pools and production assets along the value chain because one thing is certain: these too will have to be geared toward consumer benefit.

Digitized value chains define the overall benefit for the consumer—from the bean plant to enjoying a coffee or from the ore mine to the ultimate mobility service. The ultimate end customer benefit need not necessarily be equated with the final product here.

### Significance for the Manufacturing Industry

The manufacturing industry is about to embark on an enormous learning curve. The key objective is to interact with one another as a chain. Industry 4.0 refers to the challenge of linking and optimizing value chains—beyond company borders too. New business models will go on to be shaped by these parameters. It is not just

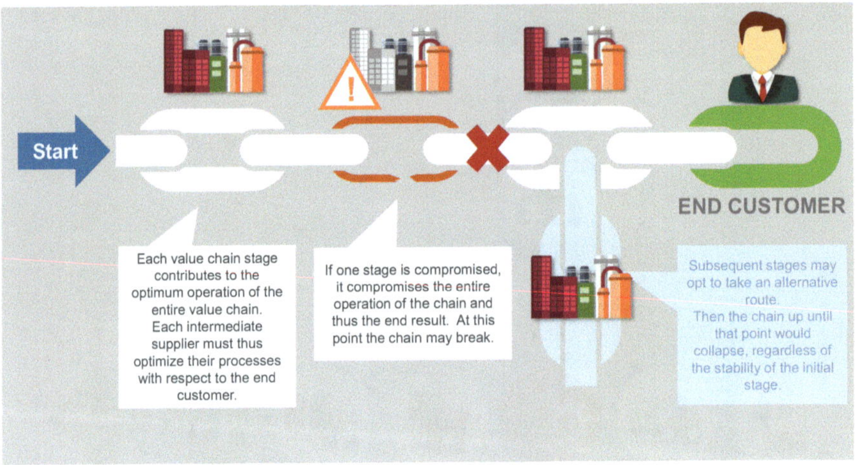


**Fig. 2.6** Impacts on the value chain

collaborative development that is called for. All elements of the value chain need to move closer together. After all, digitized value chains are only as robust and strong as their weakest link (see Fig. 2.6). Each value chain stage contributes to the optimum operation of the entire value chain. That means that everyone must participate actively in the change. Even intermediate suppliers must optimize their processes with regard to consumer benefit.

At the interface with the customer is where the pitfalls of digitized value chains lurk. The ability to understand the consumer benefit, to draw the right conclusions and offer the right product requires new expertise not necessarily present in today's B2C companies. The ability to gather information on a broad basis is a must at this sensitive point within digitized value chains. The value of this information should not be underestimated and can be likened to that of commodities. This information can help determine what should be supplied when, in what quality, and where. These kinds of processes are already a reality in the retail trade. Distribution giants top up the shelves as and when products are required. Intelligent services delivered by fast and flexible companies could soon see today's B2C companies—usually big players in their sectors—swept aside on the market. They will disappear along with their classic ways of thinking. Alleged technological entry barriers no longer apply, neither do 30 years' supplier experience. Distinct benefits identified by information seek products. That is why it pays to gear your own value chain towards the customer benefit.

## Disruption

The courage to make difficult—and often expensive—decisions is becoming a fixed part of digitized value chains. This is where companies are left open to attack. For example, if a company has invested in a 30-ton press system 2 years ago, then it will do everything it can to develop its value chain on the basis of the new system. Even if the investment decision was right at that point in time, past decisions are not the measure of all things. Developing products around a 30-ton press will not help to deliver consumer benefit, what matters is relevance to customer needs. It only makes sense to digitize production facilities and network across company boundaries where this is in the interests of the relevant benefit. Companies must learn to gear their enterprise's transformation toward the consumer—regardless of any investments made, regardless of prior experience, and regardless of previous partnerships.

Our economic system currently finds itself in a situation where ample investor capital is available on the market. This means there should be funding available for whatever new trend comes along. And where inventive genius meets capital, global players can emerge. Competing companies are the driving force behind competition. Those who learn how to understand, accept, and respond to change fast enough will gain ground on the competition when it comes to designing new business models.

Data-driven services refer to a model that describes the changes involved with digitized value chains and demonstrates which specific changes will result for companies. It provides food for thought as to the direction in which organizations, companies, and people can (must) develop and what the first steps in the transformation process might look like. The key question with regard to everything from even just the asset life cycle, the supply chain model right through to the data-driven service model is changing. Now businesses are asking themselves: how can I as a company, department, or individual gear structures and investments toward the ultimate consumer benefit? Individual product parameters and the quantity price variable are increasingly regarded as obsolete in response to this question.

Changes in the claim to leadership are an inevitable consequence of all data-driven services since it is people who initiate change. The impact of these changes is too much for classic corporate developments. Change is becoming a daily companion, driven not by trends, but by technological possibilities. Organizations must now learn and practice the skill of permanent adaptability. The aim of this process must be to allow the organization a high degree of flexibility because that is exactly what managers must teach their organizations: adaptability: This is the only way companies can ensure that their value chains are permanently geared toward the consumer.

# The Digital Revolution Is Everywhere

# 3

Digitalization is producing vast amounts of data +++ Why data protection is becoming almost impossible +++ Data is a major source of untapped potential for business +++ Why customer benefit should be the key focus for companies +++ Digital transformation is the key to the future viability of our companies +++

Calls for data security are becoming less and less with the exponential increase in data volumes. Politics, industry, and individuals are coming to the realization that there is no such thing as absolute data security. Any attempts to pursue this would be destined for failure. There are no barriers to the decryption of data, and there is no absolute guarantee that data will not end up in the hands of third parties. Countless disclosures, data leaks, and whistleblowers have taught us this. This may raise a few eyebrows among data protection officers but, the fact remains, the flow of data will not be stemmed. As long as a person functions in day-to-day life, as long as he/she takes part in society, he/she will produce and transmit data—and never confidentially. In the microseconds it takes for information to pass the threshold between reality and virtuality, it is digitally encoded, i.e., converted into the digits 0 and 1, allowing it to flow through every inch of the World Wide Web. This data can be tangibly measured, displayed, and reproduced. Using algorithms data can be decrypted on all levels of being: location, time, state, and intention; even the needs, and emotions and desires of the transmitter contain this code, thus transforming data into an abundant source that fuels industry too. This realization has led to a more moderate tone. People are no longer calling for security but protection. Individuals are entitled to the protection of their data. Their data is, after all, part of their personal freedom.

But how can this protection be effective? This is one of the key questions of our modern times, where information quantities are reaching volumes beyond our



A. Weber, *Digitalization for Value Creation*, Future of Business and Finance,
https://doi.org/10.1007/978-3-030-36229-4_3

human imagination. With trust in politics and good company leadership in the economy at an all-time low, things could be better. But individuals have a responsibility to demonstrate self-aware conduct too. One simple tick next to the terms of use on social networks or other online platforms in the sectors of communication, commerce, health, banking, etc., means a loss of control over what happens with the data collected subsequently. Every individual should be aware of the fact that by downloading an app, paying by card at a counter, accessing public spaces, using modes of transport, consulting doctors, they are providing information about their habits, preferences, needs, illnesses, etc. Everyone should therefore be aware of the consequences or leaving a data trail. And question who they allow insight into their thoughts and emotions.

Only those who assess what brings them benefit and what is dispensable remain in control of their data. The benefit starts where people, as customers, receive custom services and ends where absolutely no added convenience is identifiable. I will use the following example to highlight this personal responsibility: We want maximum security on national and international flights. Yet, inwardly, we balk at the fact that face recognition is matched up with worldwide databases when we board an aircraft. The line between emotional feeling of freedom and rational security considerations is a thin one—and everyone must decide for themselves where the line is. The key is to develop awareness in relation to data—and what can be done with it.

## 3.1 The Smartphone: The Data Vacuum

Equipped with physical sensors, smartphones can now measure heat, acceleration, and vibration with the assistance of apps. They are capable of determining the geographical position of the user, recording their voice, and saving biometric data such as fingerprints. In time each detail comes together to form an individual profile, an everyday reality that is measurable, scalable, and predictable. Phone calls are of secondary importance here. The steps the user takes, the vigor with which they appear, the journeys they take, the positions they transmit, take center stage. Each photo is marked with a date, time, and location, every website visited, and every contact saved in whichever form. These small, seemingly incidental gestures come together to create a transparent profile. Users transmit data incessantly without thought, revealing what they would conceal in a face-to-face discussion: information about their fitness, their metabolism, their biorhythm, and their sleeping and waking habits. They are in continuous contact with GPS and Galileo satellites and an integral part of the global network. Now—subject to relevant app usage—they transmit information in the form of data to the systems of banks, insurance companies, authorities, and various branches of industry. While privacy is shrinking to an ever-greater extent, data output is exploding.

Being in control of your own data is part of the subsidiarity that a democracy allows its citizens. This requires an informed and future-minded way of thinking and awareness of the impact of today's actions tomorrow.

It is a question of shaping this future consciously but with curiosity and effortlessness too. In my opinion there are three indispensable rules for handling your own data:

1. Data protection begins with carefully reading all the terms and conditions that need to be accepted before using smartphones, fitness trackers, apps, or participating in online communities. If you have any doubts about a provider's integrity, you should avoid the app in question.
2. Question the rationale behind an app and estimate how much and what information you intend to reveal while using it. Where is the acceptable limit of transmitted data, and what environment are you operating in by downloading an app, joining a chatroom, or authorizing your data on a social network?
3. Consider the benefit and effect. What benefit do you get in exchange for transmitting sensitive data? Always assume that any data could be hacked, regardless of any encryption promises.

The industry has an undisputed interest in obtaining customer data. It can, for example, use it to identify trends, create custom services for specific customers, or it can develop ideas for new products or business models based on user activity. The challenge lies in pushing the pace while at the same time allocating the customer the central role in your strategy. The aim should be to form a triad between data protection, data exchange, and data use. If a company wants to acquire customer data, it should know that the customer expects an added benefit in return. Any companies generating customer data must ensure the sensitive handling of this data—and that they demonstrate transparency in their dealings vis-à-vis the customer. Nothing more and nothing less.

## 3.2 Hesitation at the Expense of the Customer

Nokia's launch of the Communicator 9000 in August 1996 marked the beginning of the commercial smartphone era. For the first time ever, a device—created for managers—was offering fax, e-mail and organizer functions and Internet access to boot. At roughly 2700 DM, the price was high and very data connection incurred an extra cost. At that time the small miracle weighed heavy in jacket pockets at 400 g. But still, 361,000 units were sold, enough for Nokia to hail their entry into this future market as a success. Successor models were developed, the controls simplified, and the weight reduced; there was a pride in being a trendsetter. But sometimes pride can make you blind and that is how Nokia lost sight of the future.

It was actually the competition that sets out to revolutionize the smartphone sector by designing devices with touch screens, equipped with a camera and with a direct connection to online sales platforms for apps and music. The first iPhone surprised the competition with this all-in-one package in 2007. Customers turned their backs on Nokia after this. What is significant is that, at the time, sector insiders were the only ones to sneer at Apple's revolutionary approach of equipping the phone with just one button. The customer response, on the other hand, was overwhelmingly positive. They immediately understood the advantages that Apple's innovation had to offer. They bought the device that offered them the greater benefit—brand loyalty was no longer a relevant factor for them. Since then the iPhone has sold more than a million times.

Smartphones account for an enormous portion of global data trails. Given that these were calculated at 8591 exabytes by experts in 2015, this figure will probably be 40,026 exabytes in another 5 years (Deutschlandradio Kultur 2016). To demonstrate the sheer magnitude of this: one exabyte is made up of a trillion bytes. Three in four Germans contribute significantly to boosting this figure. That is because they own a smartphone which features constantly in their day-to-day life. A user takes their smartphone in their hand to surf, check e-mails, take pictures, or make phone calls an estimated 88 times a day. Today, communication is media driven. Traditionalists among scientists regard this development as alarming—they feel people are becoming increasingly less capable of directing their senses in the real world. They criticize the associated passivity of mirror neurons and a lack of trained empathy. But there are some opposing expert opinions who view this type of communication as enriching. The University of Mannheim launched a research project on this recently. Media and communications expert Professor Angela Keppler noted in an interview that she did not see "any great cause for alarm or negative outlook." She went on: "Change in underway, that cannot be disputed." But this new form of communication just works (Spiegel 2016).

Those who lift up their corporate visor will be able to grasp this change and use it to their advantage and to meet customer needs. Doing so does not merely involve collecting data but rather filtering, linking, and analyzing it with the help of algorithms. It is about approaching future developments not with doubt, but with an optimism that change can benefit this world. Progress depends on mindset. Had Kodak, once the giant of the photography industry, taken such a positive approach, the company would not have died a death twice over. A lot of valuable time was lost before Kodak realized that analog photography had been surpassed. The company may have been the patentee of digital photography, but this idea remained in the drawer for too long, with Kodak not wishing to compromise its own film business. It was not long before others took it a step further. In industry, waiting can often turn out to be a mistake which leads to collapse or, in the case of Kodak, even bankruptcy. Kodak did battle on, launching digital products by moving data to chips, an expensive decision in the 1990s. Chip's sensory had furthermore not yet been fully developed. Kodak conducted further research here, secured new patents, but it was already too late. Other firms, including a number of branch outsiders from the entertainment industry like Sony and Panasonic, mixed their business with the digital industry—then came the success of Smartphone manufacturers, again Apple, in particular. With the arrival of the iPhone, digital photography moved on to a smaller, lighter format and there was no longer any need to have a camera as well as a smartphone. Apple did not add the finishing touches to its models in laboratories, instead it gathered the feedback of users with just one promise: Usability and quality will be even better in the next model.

In exchange for their data trails, customers want a say in the product, an everyday benefit. That would be a win-win situation for customers and manufacturers. Up until now however, the customer has been becoming increasingly transparent and the industry is failing to take note. Data is being collected for the sake of collecting, without generating any direct benefit for the customer. The latter is taking an ever more critical view of across-the-board information scanning. But we have long been at a point where the customer can no longer avoid his or her transparency. Even if they opt not to use a smartphone since there is no identifiable benefit to them, their data sources will not simply dry up. They will bubble up elsewhere.

## 3.3 What the Sausage Packet Tells Us

Imagine you are at the sausage counter in a small store where you regularly queue up on a Saturday. You enjoy a slower pace at the weekend, avoiding the hectic atmosphere of the supermarkets. Maybe you are combining your trip to the store with a walk around the lake before looking forward to some cured sausage delicacies. So, you wait patiently in the small store for the saleswoman to ask: "What can I get for you?" To which you respond with a smile "Five smoked-cured sausages as always," only to be informed by the woman behind the counter that "those are sold out." Your smile starts to drop as you wonder: "How could that happen?" Quite simply: this store does not enter its products on a digital system. The sales receipt is stapled on by hand, or the sales assistant might well still mark the final amount directly on the packaging paper with a pencil—just like in her grandmother's time. This means that the information on who buys what and when depends solely on the sales assistant's powers of recollection. In a supermarket with a seamless production and distribution chain from manufacturer to service, with a well-functioning communication system from the meat industry and the supplier right through to the logistics provider and all service providers involved in the process, this disappointment only occurs rarely. That is because, on making a purchase, the customer leaves behind a data trail, so all those involved along the value chain know which sausage products need to be in stock at which sales location and at what time in order to serve the local customer demand.

A sausage packet can tell us more about the customer than its contents would suggest. If it is not stapled together, but sealed with a stick-on label and a barcode, then every supermarket supervisor knows, when this is scanned at the counter and transferred to the system at the latest, on which day, at which time, and in what quantity the customer requires which product. And if the customer pays by card, then these details can be linked up with personal data. Why go to all that trouble? You might ask. So fresh sausages are in stock when you ask. So that other suitable products may be offered, and the shopping experience becomes more interactive. So that your consumer and dietary behavior might act as a data source for your diet app in conjunction with a fitness tracker. The key principle remains that companies must learn how to draw conclusions from the available data, since this is information that will be of great future value, and that they start to use this data for the benefit of the customer.

Regardless of whether a customer purchases in an online store or whether they opt to visit a store: they leave behind data on their shopping habits. Do they click on different things online, do they choose products which deviate from their usual options? Are they of an age where they are likely approaching the end of their studies, launching a career, and starting a family? Or are they on the verge of retirement? Industry wants to identify all these life stages. But this will have not yet been converted into action: There is a lot of gathering and listening, as opposed to analysis and sharing—and subsequently offering beneficial products tailored to customers. Some call it caution, I suspect that behind that lies a sort of convenience, a tendency to cling on to old structures. Despite German Chancellor Angela Merkel's assertion: "Data is the commodity of the 21st Century," instigating change in the corporate and political world will require more than a wonderful metaphor. There has long been a lack of incentive to simply act!

When I look at data protection in Germany and beyond in the European community, I can safely say that enough is enough. Improvement is not necessary and drawing up angst-inducing scenarios is redundant. The industry should move within this framework and instigate change from within. It should open the lids of data silos and learn what it means to divulge data to suppliers and bring about real transformations. And the politicians? They need to recognize that there is only one formula to ensure that they do not fall behind other world leaders: improving data sovereignty but working with data. This is already being put to practice in the automotive industry.

## 3.4 Driver Profiles

Thanks to intelligent engine electronics, cars are connected to control rooms that analyze their customers' data and use it when drawing up contracts. Those who drive carelessly will fail inspections, those who compromise the lifetime of the vehicle by unnecessary wear to the clutch, abrupt gear changes, or delayed oil changes, pay. Driving behavior is not a secret, it is an encrypted formula that the vehicle manufacturer analyzes. Even dirty windshields are registered and added to the digital system. Early wear to the electronics can nullify any supposed guarantee or increase the final lease installment payment. The objection is pointless. The driving behavior log also supplies insurance agencies with cases. Anyone predicted to be at likely risk of an accident will not get an insurance policy. The car owner whine and promise to improve as much as he wants, Big Data is a credible source for case processors, even a guideline for action. The fact that this almost seamless data link can also function as a theft deterrent is a welcome development for the police given that enabled tracking systems allow any route to be traced in real time, provided the system has not been hacked or compromised by the thief or the car has not yet been loaded into an aluminum container, causing it to disappear from the data radar.

Full sector digitalization has led to new business models: the modern version of carsharing. A customer allows companies like DriveNow to monitor all their movements and to analyze their driving behavior. The higher regional court of Cologne recently confirmed this customer surveillance to be legal and not in violation of data protection (Chip 2017).

These companies have adopted a farsighted attitude and recognized that customers want more than simply to rent a car on an hourly or daily basis. They have asked themselves: what will the customer of tomorrow want? To move through cities independently and when they want. To take one single route between two appointments without having to return to the place of collection to hand back the car. They want the spontaneous and flexible availability of a car without having to seek out a service desk at a fixed location. To put it bluntly: they want to jump in, drive away, arrive and go, without having embarked on a complicated hunt for branches, fill out forms, and without having to leave a form of identity every time.

If car rental firms that still operate over-the-counter communications fail to change their business model, in 5 years' time they will cease to exist.

## 3.5 160 l Water for a Cup of Coffee?

Such new business models, enabled by digitalization in the first place, offer the customer added value in the quality of life and save them time. But data analysis is capable of far more, particularly if Big Data starts to be used on a large scale: If conflict breaks out somewhere in the world, a search on Google and the outcry on social media brings this to our attention long before peace research institutes label it a conflict. If a gastrointestinal virus is spreading throughout a region, notices are supplied online far quicker than health boards can distribute them thanks to the data generated. Why, given the immense advantages, are digital business models still the exception rather than the rule in Germany? Companies, authorities, and organizations lack digitalization strategies. A lack of strategy will make it very difficult to exploit the opportunities of the digital revolution.

Real-time data analysis has the ability to improve our lives, in some cases even save them. It even has the ability to contribute to saving finite resources. This requires looking at the entire value chain and thinking far outside the box: If 160 l of water is required for one single cup of coffee in the entire production chain, then a reduction of this amount to, say, 120 l would be a considerable step forward given the impending water scarcity on our earth. This could succeed if companies and organizations were willing to share their data transparently and responsibly. This can work in a compliant system, where companies are free to talk about and exchange their data. This can work if, in this era of digitalization, we cast aside anachronistic legislation, e.g., anti-trust barriers, in the interests of networking, provided this serves the environment and people.

Back in the 1970s, nobody would have believed that the computer would have become as powerful a feature of everyday life as it is, nobody would have expected the smartphone to become such a force for communication on every level. But it happened. Now Microsoft is capable of accurately anatomically depicting the human brain—one of the last remaining secrets of this world—with the help of an app. Three-dimensional graphic depiction allows us to look into the depths of this fascination and register the activities in the different parts of the brain as well as their links. This app is an educational module in medical neuroanatomy. Google is working on the development of self-driving cars. These are guided by satellite-controlled tracking systems as well as assisted by 3D cameras and ultrasound-based 360-degree detection systems. What may be in 20 years time may be beyond the powers of our imagination.

Those who dare to contemplate a future in the field of digital research will discover new system architectures that are self-refining and self-learning. Thanks to exponentially increasing computing capacity they will use algorithms on a meta level and might even help to overcome language barriers 1 day. They will identify forms of artificial intelligence which, thanks to objective analysis, may even be capable of interpreting emotions. They will maybe even see NASA's dream of a space highway between the moon and the earth become a reality, where flying cars hurtle along as if they were shuttling between one city and another.

We should entertain these future visions, not shy away from them—even if they are still unimaginable. We should go with time's arrow. It is too late now to turn back anyway, time's arrow has been moving forward since time immemorial, only now it is surging forward faster than ever since the invention of the Internet.

## 3.6 Glimpse into the Future

As a manager, imagination is required. Industry 4.0 is, after all, a highly creative process that requires three things: first of all, enthusiasm, secondly expertise and thirdly the courage to act. When considering total personnel development budgets and their allocation, it strikes me how much industry invests in the training and further education of its managers. This is disproportionately higher than investment in staff members. A big mistake! In this era of *sharing* and a shared adoption of responsibility, it is no longer a question of the chief calling and the Indians following command. The industry needs open-minded, creative staff who are willing to learn. It needs people that really get stuck into their projects and never tire of developing scenarios that seem *spacey* enough to be fresh out of a science fiction film.

Together in your team, ask yourselves the magic question: What would happen if entire value chains no longer featured any person-to-person communication, if not one single word was spoken from the idea and the product right up to stocking in-store, but simply machine-to-machine communication? What would happen if, in the process, data was analyzed in real time and made available to all machinery involved in the interests of further optimization? What would happen with the employees who perform these tasks simply because they speak, decide, and act? Think outside the box. And above all: think positively. This is, after all, the only way to arrive at productive results.

So, hear my plea: if the digital transformation is to succeed, then there is only one thing which should be invested in staff. Maintenance, services, personnel, distribution, and marketing: Every operational unit in a company, from managers to part-timers, shapes the digitalization process. Only when all staff are capable of seeing through the complexity of systems, creative and courageous enough to question each individual value chain stage and use their imagination to optimize it for the future, only when they decode data and view it as a life elixir, when they can predict attacks from the outside and avert these strategically, understand the language of the customer and possess an open attitude to ever-changing tasks, only then we will be on the right path.

Digital transformation should not be disregarded as an executive concern, nor should it rest in a vault full of ideas for the future. It belongs in the hands of the doers, the employees equipped with technological, service oriented, expert and communicative abilities, capable of developing an idea, and resolutely bringing it to fruition. This will see management tasks change. Managers are becoming team leads who operate on eye level with their staff. They are leaving the pyramid structures and standing with two feet on the ground—no longer residing on the top floor behind soundproof walls. Employees are becoming specialists, experts in their fields and, thus, debate participants to be taken seriously.

We are about to witness an enormous acceleration in the change process. And we must adapt to this transformation, otherwise we, as individuals, groups, companies, organizations, states, the world population will lose out. The industry has a prominent position in this list since, ultimately, it is the industry that guarantees growth and prosperity. These two factors can only be achieved if the industry makes a success of the digital transformation. The Federation of German Industry (BDI) noted the following in a study: "By 2025 Europe could achieve a growth of 1.25 billion euros in gross industrial value added, yet also suffer a 605 billion euros loss in value creation" (Roland Berger Strategy Consultants/BDI 2015).

In the following chapters, I will describe some of my practical experience gained in supervising a number of transformation processes and share with you the management instruments relevant to this. I encourage you to adapt these to your sector. I want to relieve you of any reservations you may have. Because one thing is for sure: despite the Fourth Industrial Revolution creeping up on us in stealth mode, heads will still roll. Those who do not learn to use the current opportunities to develop and embrace change, will not survive this revolution.

## References

Chip (2017) http://www.chip.de/news/Carsharing-Auto-als-Zeuge-Auto-sagt-vor-Gericht-gegen-Fahrer-aus_106982278.html. Accessed 6 Feb 2017

Deutschlandradio Kultur (2016) Smartphones & Communication. Das persönliche Gespräch stirbt nicht aus. Angela Keppler in discussion with Korbinian Frenzel. http://www.deutschlandradiokultur.de/smartphones-kommunikation-das-persoenliche-gespraech-stirbt.1008.de.html?dram:article_id=346321. Accessed 6 Feb 2017

Roland Berger Strategy Consultants/BDI (2015) Die digitale Transformation der Industrie. P. 3. Berlin. http://bdi.eu/media/presse/publikationen/information-und-telekom-munikation/Digitale_Transformation.pdf
Spiegel (2016) http://www.spiegel.de/auto/aktuell/bmw-liefert-gericht-bewegungsprofil-eines-carsharing-kunden-a-1104129.html. Accessed 7 Sept 2016

# Data Is Power

# 4

Economic and social change prevails in spite of its skeptics +++ Companies must redefine their role in the value creation chain +++ Why business models can change overnight +++ What freedom means for Industry 4.0 +++ Opening data silos means securing your future +++ Creating a win-win situation for customers and companies +++ The basis for your big data strategy +++

History has taught us that before every great change comes fear, hesitation, and reticence thanks to a fear of the unknown. In 1835, when the first steam-driven train traveled from Nuremberg to Fürth at a speed of around 35 km an hour, the 200 passengers on board feared for their lives due to the sheer speed on the tracks. Speeds were later restricted so as to save on resources. But the instinct to go further, quicker began to take root in the minds of the engineers. Today, just 150 years later, a Japanese team is working on a magnetic levitation train that will link cities at a speed of 500 km/h.

Nowadays mobility is associated no longer with fear, but curiosity about what is possible. There is an almost natural coherence between the expectations of people and the developments of time. Tempora mutantur—times change. And we change with them. This notion is apparent in the topic featured in this chapter. For the majority of people, data is an everyday and measurable phenomenon in the technologically accelerated present—but for a few others it remains above all an angst-ridden subject matter. While the latter would rather board up the windows and doors of their own private little worlds against third-party data extraction, the former are intent on using this as an opportunity for their own creativity. They know that: (1) data flows through the smallest gaps anyway and (2) data is not a physical entity and cannot be retained. They are the essence of the present and will go on to shape the megatrends of the coming decades—digitalization, mobility, globalization, ecology, heath, the environment, education, urban planning, individualization, etc. This



A. Weber, *Digitalization for Value Creation*, Future of Business and Finance,
https://doi.org/10.1007/978-3-030-36229-4_4

is precisely where I see the challenge for industry, namely breathing life into these trends by generating, analyzing, and linking data. This involves thoughts and actions in the Fourth Industrial Revolution revolving around the end customer, specifically those that provide data voluntarily, thereby fueling digitalization.

It does not take very much to obtain a customer's trust. Basically, all that required is to convey the customer that the convenience and individuality can be integrated into their life just by deciphering data. As soon as the customer can be sure that a company takes a transparent approach to handle personal data, while at the same time protecting it from misuse, he or she will allow insight into any private thoughts and thus his/her desires. The customer will express their emotion. Acquiring this knowledge can be regarded as a silver bullet, yet still, interpreting emotions is a neglected aspect of Industry 4.0. Essentially: as soon as you in your company open your data silos and allow your staff—who are far closer to the customer than you yourself—to observe, analyze, and interpret customer data, as soon as your data findings no longer relate simply to standard questions, but instead take into account a broad range of emotions, then you will start to see your customers in a different light. You will start to recognize their individual facets. Train your staff. Pay attention to the individual customer—not just the flood of data.

Getting staff on board for the mammoth task of digitalization is the key to instilling the sort of enthusiasm on which success is built. (1) Because employees can see themselves as pioneers. (2) Because they can courageously enter new territory. (3) Because true to the great words of the Austrian economist Joseph Schumpeter—"*Denke immer das Neue ins Offene!*" (loosely translated: "always dream aloud!")—they use modern tools which are often made up of data.

**Focus: Your Place in the Value Chain**

Define your role in the value creation process by asking yourself the following questions:

- Which companies are involved in your production operations?
- How does the raw material provided by all involved companies make its way to you?
- What impact does the quality of the raw materials delivered have on your value chain stage?
- What production steps are required up to the point at which the product is finished and market-ready?
- How do all subsequent steps unfold from the product logistics to the end customer?

Classic value chains such as that depicted in Fig. 4.1 are not capable of efficiently and flexibly addressing the needs of consumers. They are characterized by rigid processes: upstream suppliers deliver raw materials.

(continued)

Production starts with the assistance of the in-house logistics division. Then the items are dispatched to distributors or fabricators. They market the product and are the only participant in the value chain to have direct contact with the end customer.

Supply chains and/or value chains describe the step-by-step creation of a product for an end customer (indicated in green here). In theory, these chains start with the initial raw material and raw material logistics and lead to production (indicated in red here). Here the product is generated and delivered to the next participant in the chain, which then markets it to the end customer. These chains are more or less complex in their compositions, may feature branches and parallel branches, but always result in a final product. The raw material for production may also be the product of another.

In "classic" approaches, each link in the chain optimizes only their own value chain stage. The availability of data allows chains to be made more effective and more flexible as a whole. The avoidance of interface loses beyond company boundaries ensures added efficiency.

There are two reasons why this prompt by Schumpeter has not lost any of its appeals, popping up as a formula to counter against a corporate collapse in the digital era: First of all: companies must be inquisitive, creative, and empathetic. Secondly: entrepreneurs need to detect the blind spots within their own system. Here too, the aforementioned economist offers a clue with his well-known "creative destruction" metaphor. Companies require exactly this approach of creative self-destruction to protect themselves from disruptive attacks by the competition or completely new sector outsiders.

A company's business model can change completely overnight, the same applies to its value chain. Amazon transformed itself from an online book retailer to an online temple of consumerism and logistics provider. Google has expanded its concept of data collector to an industry player, offering navigation services, developing self-driving vehicles, driving forward development in robotics, and building drones. This has allowed Google to grow thanks to its ability to view data as a resource, to form future scenarios on the basis of this and predict human emotions.

**Fig. 4.1** Classic value chain

That is why, for companies, data is the most essential source of energy and inspiration for the future. And that is why everyone who works in these companies has an ethical obligation to analyze data with great care. Entrepreneurs who factor this approach into their strategy will not require any detailed legislation for handling the information they have acquired. They will use their freedom in the interests of value creation to enrich the market and therefore the customer and will not tire of fine-tuning the future, as outlined by the great thinker Schumpeter.

This maxim applies to all sectors of industry: machinery and plant construction, the chemicals, electronics, and automotive industry, space travel and aviation, medical and energy technology, etc. And I am tempted to say: thanks to mobile devices, chips, and cards, as well as the growing online activity of people it has never been easier to generate and analyze data. Smart factories, smart companies, smart cities, and smart homes will continue to boost data floods. Here it is a question of learning how to collate data from the various company divisions and to identify the available data, to visualize it, assess its value and, thus, to better understand value creation and ultimately the customer.

## 4.1 Freedom in the Digital Era

Advancing Industry 4.0 is also a political question. Politicians are under pressure to create a broad framework and explore all the possibilities, instead of putting up obstacles—even if future skeptics' calls for digital legislation are intensifying. This, in their opinion, would make data controllable and restrict the powers of Amazon, Facebook, and Google. Really? A law in one country will not matter one bit on the other side of the world, and data flows know no national boundaries.

In this era of accelerated digitalization freedom is returning to its roots—i.e., individual responsibility and a creative process. Freedom means dreaming up future scenarios for yourself, tapping into potential, the freedom to expand company boundaries, the ability to draw up custom entrepreneurial solutions without being restricted by standards and regulations.

No legislation can stem the flow of the data tide, nor can it determine the interpretation of information. This would be a step backward. A senseless and unfeasible endeavor. Today nobody wants to go without those benefits which, 30 years ago, sounded like a fantasy from a science fiction film, and which have now long been part of our everyday life. Voice recognition via smartphone, navigation via GPS, processing powers which, true to the prediction of Gordon Moore, so far have doubled every 18–24 months. The physicist and Intel cofounder made this bold prediction back in 1965, one that has been proven right to this day. Nowadays one chip can hold 1.3 billion transistors, that figure was 65,000 30 years ago. While some people may say that Moore's law was a self-fulfilling prophecy since the sector was making every effort to make this target a reality, there is, on the other hand, a sense of astonishment that it still applies to this day. Where do the limits of processing power and the data generated by this lie? What are the limits of performance and storage capacity in plants and machinery? We do not know—but we should be starting to leverage today's potential. Moore himself is actually said to have answered the question of limitations in 2003: "Nothing exponential lasts forever, but eternity can be postponed" (Zeit online 2015).

For critical readers it should be noted that even if the acceleration curve of processing speeds was to level out, this would have little to no bearing on the performance capacity of computers. Today, computer farms are connected in parallel x times over, to be set to one single task, verify results or develop parallel paths. These computer farms are autonomous systems that cannot be shut down. These have already reached such performances that no company would dare give these capacities free reign. Nobody can seriously claim to be able to verify these processing capacities, nor is anybody capable anymore of determining how a computer operates and makes decisions. There no limit in sight and eternity is still being delayed as Moore said.

## 4.2 No Room for Restriction

We in the European Union require a common understanding that linked-up and more efficient production must be accompanied by progressive automation and digital customer interfaces. What we need is farsightedness, not a crippling discussion about the details. Digital legislation understood in this way would make communication and information structures in the individual European countries compatible with one another, actively support digital transformation, and continue to promote investment plans in digitally networked and flexible production chains (as described in Fig. 4.1) in the interests of moving away from standardization.

In my opinion, platforms like the "Industrial Data Space" project, launched by the government in the interests of the exchange of information between science, economics, and politics, are almost completely redundant tools. Although the status quo of Industry 4.0 is yet to be determined and examined, this type of clustering does nothing but hold up processes. After all, a platform can only act as one test environment for practicing cooperation or collaboration; it will not be able to cover long-term exchange requirements.

Holding discussions and drafting scenarios are tried and tested steps toward exploring an issue, but there is a great risk of remaining in the discussion phase. By international comparison, the linking of production sites is considerably more practical and targeted. This is exactly the risk to which I refer: Germany might lose its attractiveness as a production location due to its hesitant culture.

Waiting will only serve to marginalize domestic companies. In the eyes of digital companies like Amazon, Google and Co. that have long since grasped how to create a practical data basis, this will be regarded almost as an invitation to drain data and thereby continue to assert their dominance on a giant market of possibilities. If we remain a country of doubters, continuing to groan and lament our apparent loss of freedom, we will not get anywhere because neither liberal structure nor the rule of law is compromised by digitalization. We just need to act! We can draw up general standards for handling data on our way to the digital future. Practical experience will provide us with far more material than playing through any amount of eventualities. And these are more likely to be refined by *way of doing*—in companies, in plants, on machinery, in creative rounds, in a team, at university through improved curricula, in apprenticeship places through dual courses of study—than alone in the office of any doubter.

Indeed, it is however entirely appropriate to attach a certain amount of skepticism to future optimism, just as the *FAZ* attempted to do in their culture section. "Even all the collected data of Google, Facebook and Amazon put together have not defeated cancer or halted climate change. Up until now equation hasn't quite worked out that way: free supply of data from all is resulting in unknown gains for a very few digital entrepreneurs, thereby amplifying the inequality between them and us" (Runde 2016). Correct! This is what happens when our companies look on helplessly from the sidelines, instead of exerting counter pressure with their own concepts, thus preserving their own values in the process. Data offers the basis for this. Data is available not only to the power players but to every company on the path toward Industry 4.0. It will continue to grow in abundance as the years go on—all the while offering the best means of countering a data and profit monopoly. That is why I urge you: Start monitoring and reading your data now.

Today's individual companies featuring in value chains such as that in Fig. 4.1 base all their processes and actions on the following formula alone:

$$\text{quantity} \times \text{price } D \text{ sales}$$

This remains an all-important control parameter: marketing as much as possible, as efficiently as possible at the best price to the next link in the chain. Everything companies do—from purchasing, HR administration, and quality assurance right through to marketing, is geared solely toward their own value chain stage. What happens before or afterward is more or less blocked out.

The explosion of data triggered by digitalization is seeing the emergence of completely new possibilities with regard to the $quantity \times price = sales$ equation. This can be optimized across company boundaries thanks to data collected along the entire value chain. The crucial control parameter for a company is no longer its own value chain stage but the efficiency of the entire value chain.

This formula applies to industry, service providers, nongovernmental organizations, associations, anyone who contributes to the economy in any way and means the following in the context of digitalization: considering your role with regard to the entire value chain and not just one individual value chain stage, as has been the case previously. That is why my model is based on just one thing—from corporate strategy through to the maintenance of production plants—the correlation of all company data within the context of the overall value chain right through to the end customer benefit. This perspective will carry you forward from focusing solely on profitable growth within your own company and boosting performance indicators. It will lead you to other questions that will change your decisions and strategies: Today's demand is determined by the customer, both in the manufacturing industry and every company.

**Focus: Prepare for the Future**
The biggest challenges for the future are:

- To learn how to understand your value chain right down to the smallest detail.
- To identify where your chain is vulnerable to the outside.
- To identify the weakest link in the chain a whole.
- To assume that there is guaranteed to be an easier, cheaper, and higher quality company that can replace one of your value chain steps.
- To adopt the word disruption in your daily vocabulary given that, in the future, competition is set to be characterized by this approach.
- To include the following sentence in your guiding principles: "Decide not on the basis of yesterday's decisions, but on the basis of tomorrow's benefits."

Digital, i.e., networked, use of your data will transform your business model and, with it, your business image:

- You will be able to calculate quantity × price at each individual value chain stage.
- You will learn how to assess the cohesion of the individual stages and their impact on the entire value chain.
- You will come to recognize the analysis of your data as a means of defense against disruptive attacks.
- You will learn that digitalization requires a perfect balance of knowledge and creativity.

Any business model may be called into question overnight or even sidelined if the imagination of a competing company extends beyond your own. For example, detergent manufacturers could lose their livelihood if digitally controlled, industrial-scale launderettes were to collect their customers' shirts right from their door with the prompting of an app before delivering the shirts washed and ironed to any desired location an hour later. Such disruptive business models generally come from the intelligent linking up of insight and experience combined with the recognition of customer needs. Customers welcome this—and, in turn, are willing to disclose even confidential and secret requirements via modern communication channels—if they can see a benefit to themselves.

## 4.3 A Change of Perspective

While talking about your own salary was a no-go in Germany 30 years ago, today people have no scruples about uploading their CVs online and discussing hobbies, preferences, and personal characteristics. Generation Y and beyond, in particular, see no risk in the data trails that they leave in their wake. Furthermore, they recognize the benefit of online collaboration since it makes their everyday lives easier. What is more, data can serve the push for the individualization they so badly want. These demands explain the current freedom of data. A study by the EMC Corporation on "The Digital Universe" predicts that "the digital universe will have reached 44 billion gigabytes by the year 2020" before posing the all-important question immediately afterward: "How can you use this data to make your company more competitive" (FEMC Digital Universe 2014)? There should be no political resistance to finding an entrepreneurial response here! There should be no hesitation on the part of the industry. In fact, you should draw up a round of questions that goes beyond the usual standards of data handling and which employees should be obligated to answer:

- How can you decode user-generated data from smartphones, smart TVs, tablets, devices, chips, cards, and sensors to the benefit of people and the environment and in such a way as to lift society and the economy?
- How can you generate more benefits for your customers in the future?
- How can you succeed in decrypting the data behind the data and thereby leverage hidden potential? Data correlations can help events to be anticipated and thus better decisions made ahead of time.
- How can you optimize your value chain stages with a view to boosting quality, protecting the environment, and meeting your social responsibility as an entrepreneur?
- How can detailed checks be incorporated within the individual value chain stages in order to ensure an agile and flexible reaction to mistakes?
- What probability should you use in your calculations and what tools do you have to counter these mistakes?
- What can your company do to serve the needs of customers?
- How can you design your processes to meet the requirements and expectations of these customers?
- How can you use the availability of data to gain in-depth familiarity with the needs of your customers and convert the insights gained into algorithms to help you ensure you do not bypass the market but keep your finger on the pulse of time?
- How can you replicate your data and simplify algorithms to make them accessible to sub- and supplier companies?
- Do you know where the value chain in which you deliver is vulnerable to new technologies or solutions?

Answering these questions will be an ongoing task in Industry 4.0 and of the utmost significance to the performance of a company. But this starts with taking the first step.

## 4.4 Open Your Data Silos!

Do not wait for politics, the economy, or science to present you with the big strategy. In actual fact this will probably never happen because the complexity of detail is growing with data volumes, because algorithms change, because trends are short-lived phenomena, and because technologies will overtake your creativity before you can put it to paper. The only option is for you as an entrepreneur to embark on the digitally driven path yourself—taking your employees with you. Huge amounts of data are already available but have yet to be put to practical use. These are stored for specific purposes but never linked up in the interests of the wider benefit. Sometimes this happens as a result of misunderstood data protection reasons. Often however data is shut in silos away by individual employees because they want to use it as superior knowledge for their own marketing purposes, true to the motto: "knowledge is power." Data is generally gathered on a very specific basis and, unfortunately, only considered in the context of this specific environment. This data cannot be linked up if its existence and the valuable information it contains remains the superior knowledge of individuals.

## 4.5 Digital Behavior of Employees

Before I as an entrepreneur or manager order each individual employee to do all they can to progress digital transformation in companies, I would like to point out that, first, a digital leadership should be established. After all: Digitalization is a top-level issue. It requires a new kind of management expertise, whereby collaboration in social networks is possible, where online-based communication—both internal and external—is established, where project implementation is managed across departments. German bosses have difficulties with this, those of the older generation, in particular, worry that transparency undermines their claim to leadership and management expertise. But there is no longer any place for such reservations in modern management. Industry 4.0 has lean structures, breaks up pyramidal organigrams, and makes departmental boundaries penetrable. Only when managers dispose of their own little vanities can the digital spark be passed on to staff. Digital transformation is more than just a technological upgrade for hardware and software. It is based on the idea of collecting and connecting data and drawing ground-breaking conclusions from this. Each individual within a company can make their own contribution, and should for practicality's sake, preach, and live this new transparency.

Regardless of age, role, or corporate affiliation, employees must face this change in approach to work and values with an intrinsic curiosity. And the top priority is knowing the end customer and serving the needs of tomorrow today. Each employee should gain an understanding that data is not an anonymous viscous mass, but that behind each piece of information hides a whole string of emotions that can be decoded. Every indication, however small, should feature in a corporate communications line that passes through all departments: through occupational health, logistics, HR, quality management, sales, and marketing. Data within companies is not the superior knowledge of departmental managers but a common entrepreneurial resource. Because only by sharing and analyzing data can the customer benefit be determined—and therefore the quantity × price-based sales increased for the entire value chain. Smart companies have recognized this link. They are capable of maximizing the individual value chain stages and predicting declines and growth within the asset life cycle (product life cycle). They call on their staff to share data and teach them that transparency should not be equated with job loss but new creative freedoms.

The change process starts with open-mindedness on the part of employees. In other words: causalities are identified on a technology level in the individual value chain stages, silos are opened, data interpreted, and knowledge shared intelligently. In the future, employees who fail to understand this will find that they no longer have a place in the industry given that processes can only be optimized and predicted by means of data and its analysis. If a detergent manufacturer buys in scarce raw materials or receives lesser volumes due to a natural disaster, this information has implications right up to the last stage of value chain. In a word: the customer will not receive the product in the accustomed quality or only for a considerably higher price. A decline in quality in the first stage will result in a decline in sales or a damaged image. Only through an unbroken flow of information will it be possible to respond promptly and flexibly, to look for other raw material sources or suspend and pause production ahead of time: simulating controllers, correlating capacity utilization, predicting output—that is the causality that data supplies. If this data linkage can then be mixed with the creative imagination of employees in terms of the everyday reality for end customers, we will have come to a huge step forward in the digitalization process. Employees must learn to interpret the correlations that they see and to draw the right conclusions from these. They must play with data and be able to ask themselves where they can get the information to answer questions that, so far, have gone unanswered. They must understand that this information has value and to appreciate this value—in order to protect it, but also, to market the potential of this value.

The logical next step in the detergent industry would be to provide bottles with an NFC chip to communicate with the customer's smartphone: Before the bottle is empty, a new one is placed in their basket in the online store (see Amazon push button)—and delivered following order via voice recognition. A small service, rewarded by the data the customer provides. A win-win situation. The customer receives convenient information and service, and, in return, they communicate their laundry routine, thus providing a little more insight into their day-to-day life. They disclose their electricity and water consumption, allow speculation about any sports played or holidays taken, indicate how often their washing machine runs and at what

**Fig. 4.2** Change in purchasing and sales behavior associated with the use of networked technology

time of day and when this cycle is disrupted. It is the data behind the data that is exciting for companies. It takes a little imaginative power to identify and assess this to bring the profile of the customer into even sharper focus. Companies would then, for example, know when they have to deliver which products, how these should be processed and how the benefit to the customer can be boosted in general.

The future of the industry has already arrived in some sectors (see Fig. 4.2): the use of networked technology makes it possible to react to the needs of the consumer quickly and effectively.

The insurance and banking sector is already using this type of detail analysis and digital data linking. If a company runs into difficulties, the banks already know before performance indicators are even presented in credit applications. They make their assessment based on observations of account movements, compliance with payment terms and, ultimately, their data-based score. If an insurance holder reports water damage from a storm, then the departments of the insurance company know on the basis of weather and geodata whether this damage claim is justified or not. Data transparency speaks truths. This too may be an indicator of a change in values: Only those who act credibly, transparently, and unambiguously vis-à-vis their business partners and customers and those who grasp the overall process as the sum of lots of smaller details will achieve long-term success because they have succeeded in anchoring a first Big Data strategy in their company based on findings obtained.

## 4.6 The Three Big Data Strategy Phases

Generally speaking it takes 4–6 years to implement a digitalization strategy in the industry. The goal is to use and analyze data in a practical and cross-departmental manner. This happens in three phases.

The *first phase* involves taking stock honestly. It begins with the question: "How digital are we at the moment?" Unfortunately, this question is often pushed onto the IT department with the request: "Draft a paper on this and make a note of which technologies we need." That is the wrong approach. Each and every department is responsible for the digital process. Everyone in the company is asked when they communicate which working step digitally rather than analogously and which tools are used for this. An overall assessment usually delivers the surprising insight that there is more digital work underway than expected, that data is already used as a basis for concepts and their implementation. It collects as if in a massive boiler and generates pressure because it increases year-on-year. It is often only the key to utilizing this potential that is lacking. Enlisting an external consultant is an effective solution in this initial phase. But everything that follows is an internal challenge that the manager can only overcome together with his or her team.

There is also a justified need for reflection and thus the following question: "What have we already tried and implemented to no effect?" This evaluative question is of great significance in a fast-changing environment. Technology has now changed and things that once were only moderately effective now work, are easier or cheaper to implement, fit in better with the current general opinion and are more accepted.

In the *second phase* entrepreneurs themselves will be required to open the data silo, analyzing and linking data together with the mid-management of all departments and subsequently explaining the value of the data to all staff members. This will see the working direction flow from top to bottom, from CEO to the general management staff to the coworkers. The direction is top to bottom, from CEO to staff. Ask yourself whether your internal control mechanisms are still applicable and practical in a changed world. Look for data earmarked for a specific purpose and check whether it could be of value to anyone else. Here you must consciously ask yourself whether there could be interested parties externally—as long as this does not compromise your corporate objective, you can and should market and share this information too.

The *third phase* should see your digitalization strategy unfold, until such a point as every single employee has inhaled it like entrepreneurial guidelines until it becomes a model within which everyone can find their place and role. Lively exchange is the order of the day. After all, only the perspectives of managers in the human resources, technology, security, quality, and logistics divisions will offer an insight as to how change is reflected at specific points along the entire process chain.

If you discover that you dispose of the right data sources and tools to optimize the chain, your business model will change automatically. Develop emerging potential and draft the strategy you want to employ for this future. Implementing a plan of action triggers a change in the values of a company, forming a model whereby data and tools are used to optimize in-house value creation. Many companies today are already storing consumer data on a massive scale without gaining any benefit from it.

The quantity of packaging material used can, for example, help to shed light on the efficiency of a plant. This, or stocktaking all the data stored, is the first step toward a gradually unfolding digitalization strategy (see Fig. 4.3).

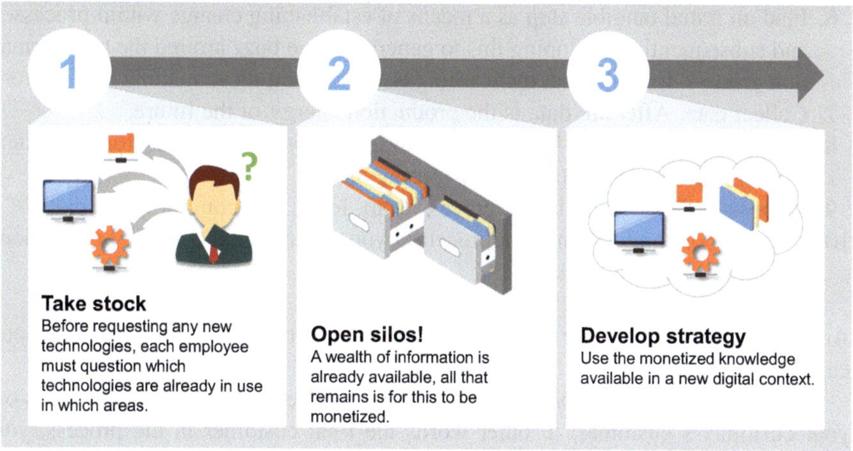


**Fig. 4.3** Launching a promising new Big Data strategy for industry involves three basic steps

Anchoring this openness within the overall process will be a significant point in the course of changing the values in the company. I have found the following plan of action to be a practical and expedient approach in many discussions.

## 4.7 Ten Points for the Initial Digital Audit

1. Open data silos—use the data flows. Leverage hidden potential.
2. Scrutinize the value creation process, predict attacks at various value chain stages and remember: any weakness at the first stage will have implications right up to the last stage. Implement practical changes immediately and involve your staff in this.
3. Is your business model under attack? Find out when and where it is happening. Your data is the instrument of choice for this:
   (a) What information have you gleaned from the value chain?
   (b) If you were to look in at the relevant value chain stage from the outside, how would you arrange elements with a view to achieving the ultimate benefit? Learning how to read the data available to you will help you to answer these questions.
   (c) What do you know about the finished product or the benefit that the customer stands to gain from the finished product? What is your contribution to this?
4. Make decisions not based on the past, but the future benefit. Change begins with those who dare to take the first step.
5. Make this clear to your employees, so as to remove any reservations they may have in relation to digitalization.

6. Find an initial tangible step as a means of establishing change within processes and subsequently developing this to generate some buzz around the transformation process. It is all about the learning effect and setting something into motion.
7. Collect data. After all, data is the production energy of the future.
8. Collaboration is smart. Do not forget to involve your subcontractors, supplier, partners, and service providers by sharing data.
9. Map out 30% of your change process, start, learn, and commit to the path!
10. Adopt a bold and visionary approach in your creations, technology is far more advanced than you think.

And above all: make clear any benefits of your actions to your staff and your customers.

With respect to the last point (10), you might argue that if you were to focus on your customer's customer, in other words the final customer in the process, you would soon run into compliance difficulties in Germany, given that your strategy would run counter to antitrust law—i.e., ultimately you would have to discuss quantities and prices across extended stretches of the value chain, thus running the risk of being regarded as anti-competitive. This is a justified concern. I see this difficulty too, and the growing number of regulations associated with this may hamper digital transformation in the industry in 4 or 5 years. If such regulations do impede the digital transformation process, we stand to lose out as a production location. If this happens, companies will choose other locations, i.e., wherever technology is seen as an advantage and a user-oriented perspective a central pillar of business models. This would see Asian countries enter a league of their own, given the freedom to optimize their value chain stages, and Germany remains stuck at the discussion stage. That is why I would urge you not to waste your energy as an entrepreneur and limited time on an endless discussion. You need a model that is easy to implement and one your employees will comply with. Take the first step, push the limits of what is possible and find out how far you can go and what stops you. Then we as a society, policy-makers, economy, consumer and data protectors and customers will learn how to modify control and regulatory tools for the greater good.

You are part of a networked chain of production operations which, at some point, will sell a product to an end customer. The following diagram—applicable to all sectors and markets—illustrates this clearly: The model in Fig. 4.4 outlines a simplified value chain with linked-up production structures, whose series-connected plants (assets) serve in the interests of overall optimization. On the vertical plane, the process engineering division lays the foundations for the planning and setup of a plant required for manufacturing the product. Even the decommissioning of the machinery has been taken into account. The horizontal plane offers a schematic view of the value chain as outlined in Fig. 4.1. Real value chains are considerably more complex.

The relevance of networked cross-company optimization becomes apparent when it comes to tailoring all these elements to one another. The aim is to achieve the

**Fig. 4.4** Simplified value chain with linked-up production structures

flexibility and efficiency in the horizontally depicted value chain that an outsider would have, were it to serve the end customer without all the existing elements.

## References


FEMC Digital Universe with Research & Analysis by IDC (2014) Das digitale Universum. https://germany.emc.com/leadership/digital-universe/index.htm. Accessed 7 Feb 2017

Runde M (2016) Wider die Fremdbestimmung – Wir brauchen ein Digitalgesetz". Frankfurter Allgemeine Zeitung. http://www.faz.net/aktuell/feuilleton/debatten/die-digital-debatte/digitalisierung-wir-brauchen-ein-digitalgesetz-14391040.html. Accessed 7 Feb 2017

Zeit Online (2015) 50 Jahre Moore's Law – Ein Grundsatz, der die IT-Branche seit 50 Jahren antreibt. http://www.zeit.de/digital/2015-04/moorsches-gesetzcomputerchip-50-jahre. Accessed 7 Feb 2017

# 5 The Modern Value Chain Stage Architecture

The customer is becoming part of the value chain +++ Why linking up the entire value chain is so important +++ How the role of the employee is changing with digitalization +++ Cooperation is better than isolation +++

Digitalization is no longer a trade secret, now it is embedded in a broad network of different actors. And this networking, based on data and the linking of data, has seen the emergence of a new value stage architecture: The focus is no longer simply on optimizing the value chain stage of one specific company, but rather each individual stage within the chain.

The sole focus of Industry 4.0 is the intelligent linkup of the individual steps between product development, production, logistics, marketing, end customers, and recycling. This is the only way to succeed in countering the difficult competitive conditions resulting from increasing volatility on markets, high commodity prices, and shorter production cycles. This will see industry know-how become the purpose of collaborations, expanding any ideas and action beyond corporate boundaries. Products are public knowledge from the developmental to the launch stage. They can be attacked, even destroyed—almost overnight. Disruption is already part of day-to-day life in Industry 4.0. While this may have been the exception rather than the rule or a more slowly emerging phenomenon 30 years ago, now it happens, surprisingly, when entrepreneurs lack the creativity to dream up worst-case scenarios. Remember: while CDs replaced vinyl records as part of a gradual process, apps, on the other hand, overwhelmed the music industry by exploding onto the market. What is next? That is the question that nobody in any sector seems to be able to get around.

Accept that your business model is no longer future proof, that it probably will not survive the next 6 years. Be adaptable! Instill in yourself and your staff the following key statement: the new architecture of flexible, digitally supported value chain stages described above aims to achieve technological, communicative, and



A. Weber, *Digitalization for Value Creation*, Future of Business and Finance,
https://doi.org/10.1007/978-3-030-36229-4_5

emotional perfection on all stages with a view to securing the entire chain. The good news is that data storage media, data analysis systems, and mobile realization devices are affordable and easy to install. Something that will be considerably more difficult is encouraging your staff to breathe life into this industrial future, turning the interaction of technology, people, and companies into a model for success. Exciting times lie ahead; Industry 4.0 has only just begun, with the customer as a key protagonist.

## 5.1 Customers as Part of Supply Chain Management

Customers are better informed than ever before. They rarely go in for sales pitches and have no time for sales statistics. The customer wants the best the market has to offer—and maybe an added perk too. If you cannot deliver this, then they will look to see what the competition has to offer—placing their order at the click of a mouse. At that very second, you disappear from the picture, visually and emotionally—in all likelihood never to appear again.

The loss of a customer is no small matter—even if this customer alone does not account for any substantial sales. But in this digital era, one single click can add up to a five-figure sum within the space of just a few hours. One single tweet expressing dissatisfaction can go viral on an international scale. Many a company has ended up in crisis in the wake of incidents like this. Customers turn to their smartphone or tablet to share their dissatisfaction in the world of social networking. Where feelings such as exasperation, irritation, anger, or disappointment play a role, adrenaline runs high and looks for a vent—in this case damaging your entire company. Whether such complaints relate merely to a broken fastening or momentarily reduced quality as a result of a lack of raw materials is of little importance to the customer. They view your product as a whole and not in individual detail, making your image worthless in their eyes. Disappointed customers spread negative experiences, that is just the way the human mind works now. Once the pain center has been triggered once, multiple positive experiences are required to erase all traces of this minor incident, sometimes it never works. Slowly this message is starting to get through to companies, leading management to the realization that: the customer is part of supply chain management, and therefore an opportunity in the value chain. Companies can use them to learn what it can do better in the future. Modern architectures require a focus on every stage of the chain because a miscalculation at one point can have a domino effect on subsequent stages. A suboptimally organized chain within a network can have devastating consequences. Ask yourself:

- Who is involved in the product?
- How can all participants communicate effectively?
- How can we progressively manage and monitor in-house processes?
- How can we guarantee the sustainable quality?

- How can we establish comprehensive occupational safety and the highest material standards?
- How can we get the product directly to the customer without any detours and ensure their satisfaction?

When Media-Saturn promises to deliver a product, whether purchased offline or online, to the customer's door within just 2 h, it caters to customer requirements—treading on Amazon's feet in the process. When Amazon launched its Prime service, with the promise of same day delivery of products to selected cities, the electronics giant let it be known across all channels that, for a small additional fee, it could top this: with delivery within an hour. Same day delivery reflects the spirit of the times, even if you have to laugh, given that Media-Saturn has already delivered the goods before the customer has had the chance to get home again after shopping in store.

## 5.2 The Time Factor in the Value Chain

The time factor plays a significant role in the digitalization era. It seems to be sped-up—but this is just an illusion. Even in the era of Industry 4.0, time remains as it always has been: a phenomenon that marches on consistently.

When *homo sapiens* first started to leave Africa an estimated 130,000 years ago, embarking on a journey of world discovery in the directions of South Asia and Australia, time moved forward at exactly the same pace at it does today. It does not multiply, not does it increase exponentially with computer capacities or for communication between machinery. It marches on just as it did when people first began to discover the earth.

But still we feel as if time is being pushed forward by the digitalization phenomenon. There is hardly anyone who does not complain about the loss of time. But it is actually the rapidly growing flood of information that is distorting our perception. We see the Surui tribe in the Amazon at breakfast. We jump time zones and connect continents. Our world is becoming more transparent, but the pulse of time remains unaffected by this. This causes confusion. This may alarm some, driving them on to increased efficiency—both in their professional and private lives. We have a 1000 goals in our mind and even more ideas for the future. We are living longer and longer. Education, knowledge, health, and peace have bought us another 30 years since the start of the last century. Are we putting it to good effect?

I am of the firm belief that, sooner or later, digitalization, the automation of tasks, the use of new technologies, and the reorganization of work will give humans exactly what they are looking for: windows of time for relaxation and reflection.

This leads us back to the all-important factor in corporate success: fulfilling the needs and requirements of the customer. Customers want to create more room for maneuver for themselves too, saving time, receiving services quicker, and deliveries faster. Thus, the time factor is always the top priority. Companies that understand this will move their logistics into alignment with this and send out a signal to the customer by saying: "We can help you to save your most precious resource: time."

Ask yourself at least once a day: When and where can I make this promise and noticeably fulfill it?

Every department in the company has a responsibility to ask itself this question. After all, this is a decisive factor in their existence, it separates today from tomorrow. Success does not come down to some large-scale strategy, but critical reflection by each member of staff as to whether their actions will contribute to an easier, more convenient everyday life for the customer. So, hear my plea: meet your staff on eye level. Talk, discuss, and open up to their ideas for improvement in the value chain stage in which they work daily. Your staff are the best experts for the job that they do. Unfortunately, managers in the industry often opt for the opposite approach, enlisting external consultants to turn the screws. This can, excuse the vehemence, be a waste of time.

## 5.3 Breathing for the Future

No external consultant will ever be able to penetrate to the core of your business. They may have the means of drafting a strategy over broad lines but when it comes to the details, your staff can bring their specialist knowledge and tangible experience to the table, enabling the future feasibility of this strategy.

Your staff know all the companies and partners involved in their value chain stage personally, they know about their working methods, preferences, and, moreover, the sticking points that can impede a process. Make it your mission to view your staff as key players. "What do we have to do today to make us the most successful company in the world tomorrow—and what can each individual company contribute to this?" Steve Jobs asked his staff similar miracle questions when he asked them to "make a dent in the universe." Too big of an ask? Not at all. Intellectual games like this are motivational incentives because they give each employee the importance they deserve and, secondly, tell them: "You are a part of this process and you can make things happen with your expertise and your creativity. Let's go!"

In a future business model, employees will ask themselves what means and tools they can use to boost the success of the company. They know the benefit of their work, the value of their actions, and have the self-awareness to ask themselves: "What would happen if I wasn't here tomorrow?" I would hope that every employee is capable of mentally imaging such a future and recognizing the thin line on which they operate daily. Nobody is more secure in their job. Everything can change overnight if other companies arm themselves to attack just one stage in your value chain. Set up a defense ahead of time by putting every little detail to the test. Individual stages are gaining in significance in modern value chain architectures—the focus is no longer solely on the overall functional process. The value chain consists of individual links; keep these in mind, particularly the weakest link. A wholly optimized mode of operation will occur only when the quality of all stages has been guaranteed and once all in the company have viewed and linked up the available data. Employees must sharpen up their ability to perceive danger, they must be willing to continuously adapt their tasks to new circumstances, they must look beyond their own task area and observe and interpret the actions of upstream and downstream stages and even suppliers. Only then will it become apparent, say, that a coffee bean is being washed twice, that the resources water, energy, and time are being wasted. Only then will it become apparent that a customer has complained about a product change, because the complaint has not been blocked by an anonymous call center, instead actually reaching those responsible in the product development division.

To me, this perspective is part of digital innovation.

"We talk about a beneficial innovation because the focus is not on beating the competition, but evading it—by generating added benefit for the buyers and the company, leading to the discovery of a new as of yet unidentified market." This is taken from writings of professors of strategy W. Chan Kim and Renée Mauborgne in their bestseller *The Blue Ocean* (Kim and Mauborgne 2015) where they advise managers to say goodbye to products and services that the customer does not value. And above all: go where nobody has gone before. Swim onward into unknown waters, where the competition cannot threaten to stifle you! Blue oceans are oxygen-rich, newly discovered niches on the global markets. Those who are prepared to throw off the ballast will get there quicker. This leads me back to the modern value chain architecture: it is changing. It is becoming more flexible, more detailed, and more fleeting. It requires efficient M2M communication (*machine to machine communication*), thus redefining the task of the asset (machine) manager.

In future maintenance will no longer be done by mechanics, but highly specialized technicians who are capable of adapting machinery to the order situation. That means: modernization, networking, optimization, increasing flexibility, and even decommissioning if the market situation requires it. They will also ensure the optimum linkup of all visible and non-visible data, strip down, or upgrade storage media and guarantee data transmission speeds across the board. What was formerly the job of the IT department (ensuring data security and data flows) will lead to a level setup in modern value chain architectures, whereby maintenance personnel play just as much of a role as production developers and logisticians. This will see IT transformed from a tool to an enabler, enabling optimization of the entire value chain. IT will lose the character of a department, thus becoming an integral part of developments. I do however recommend setting up an administrative department for digitalization.

The digital transformation setup can be based in the following positions within a company:

- the CEO or
- the COO.

It can

- Represent the focal point of Industry 4.0, developing optimized value chains, designing, and organizing business models across departments and company boundaries.
- Emphasize the long-term value of the corporate strategy.

But under no circumstances should this digitalization admin department be part of the IT department.

Digitalization is, generally speaking, a top-level concern—given the inexpressible opportunities it offers for the whole company and the impending risks associated with an incorrect or half-hearted approach. The sole task of the administrative department is to achieve an understanding among staff of the philosophy with regard to the division of tasks and data networking. It should act as a mediator, communicator, and mentor in a promising process. It should be a driving force of change. It should succeed in establishing an awareness that data is a corporate asset that can be capitalized and, ultimately, a key to growth. All employees in such an organization should work toward the optimum connection of all visible and non-visible data, the continual review of these networked dataflows, the use of appropriate storage media, and the adjustment of data transmission speeds.

However, rather than setting up an administrative department, some companies tend to embark on the road toward digitalization by pooling tasks. Then everything revolves around nothing more than guidelines, discussions, and draft concepts. Enough. That leads nowhere. Creating platforms can compromise flexibility because the focus is more on working through individual points and discussing problems and, particularly in the starting phase of the digital transformation process, waters down the individual stages of the value chain. Then the whole chain is the focus—and those hidden details at small, seemingly insignificant stages are overlooked.

## 5.4 Two Digital Launch Scenarios

At the beginning of the majority of my consultancy talks I hear the following sentence: "Yes, we know that our company needs to go digital. But what is the first step? How can we start to approach digitalization without interfering in the value chain?" When I hear this comment my eyes light up, that is because I know: whoever asks this question has understood the reality. They have mentally confronted the challenges. They will not hesitate, they are sitting in the starting blocks. All they need is a tangible trigger to get up and moving.

They are likely to feel the pressure of their suppliers, perhaps they are tormented at night at the thought of losing their strongest teammates if they continue to postpone the digitalization of their processes. To him I say how much I value adaptability and that, at first, he must only pay heed to the following: Linkup a network of willing participants, collect data, and incite communication across departments. Generally speaking, that is already 30% of what digitalization requires: a data check, data transmission, and communication flow. Do you remember my 30–70 rule? The subsequent 70% will be developed through practice, reflection, interpretation, and the adaption of data, and by asking what the local optimum is for each of the value chain stages.

An entrepreneur that has understood the practicalities and benefits of digitalization for their business will not have any worries about whether or not their investment will pay off either. They will simply say to themselves that their previous tools—e.g., classic cost-benefit analysis—are no longer up to the task. The emphasis in the current situation is not on maximizing profits but simply adaptability and the associated survival in an ever faster changing world. This is summed up by the authors of the book *Price Management*:

"The company Michelin, global market leader for car tires, developed an innovative pay-per-use model to better exhaust the value-to-customer (. . .) With this model the haulage companies do not buy any tires, but instead pay based on the kilometers traveled" (Simon and Fassnacht 2008). And, quite incidentally, data is generated as to when, where, and at what speed the truck moves in the meantime.

But I also encounter other companies that are more hesitant. Even they know that within the next 3–5 years they will hit rock bottom in terms of visibility and performance. Their attitude can be expressed as follows: "We are being pushed up against a wall by our competitors. We are losing our customers. What should we do?" The cardinal sin is to first digitize customer interfaces out of fear of losing customers, and to do so before any other stage of the relevant value chain stage has been optimized or any self-transformational ability developed. This could be likened to you setting up an online pizza ordering service alongside your Italian restaurant, advertising pizzas in every conceivable variation. But digital appearances can be deceptive. Because you have neither sausage or onions in stock, all you can deliver is salami pizza—and that is if the customer is prepared to wait for 3 h for it. What happens then? The customer is going to get annoyed. As tasty as the online photo might look—if the product ordered by the customer is not immediately ready for delivery—no excuses—they will leave you. And, still, countless companies make exactly this mistake at the start of their digitalization phase: they want to bind customers to the company using surveys and idea participation. They offer the customer interactive elements on their website, even whipping up enthusiasm with augmented reality tools, giving the customer a virtual insight into the production.

I do not much like the idea of flooding the customer with product info. Before that happens, a company must first begin the digitalization in-house, analyzing, optimizing, and guaranteeing individual stages of an overall process. The rule of digitalization is: digitize internally first, then externally. Adaptability always starts from within, working outward. And by this, I do not mean neglecting the digital customer accumulation aspect. It is just a matter of rearranging the chronological order.

It fills me with confidence that managers are declaring digital communication with the customer and gaining intelligence on their living environments as a top-level matter. But let us not put the cart before the horse. Collecting customer data without a clear strategy as to how you can use this in the interests of process optimization is pointless. In spite of your best efforts, you will land up back where you started and asking yourself: How can I serve the needs of the customer? Practice on the product—not the customer. You will recall our earlier discussion about the visualization, correlation, and analysis of data. This is exactly where you should apply this. Make your team strong before you raise the expectations of your customers. Before making grand gestures to staff, i.e., "off we go, to the customer frontline," managers must be sure that their value chain can withstand this campaign.

## 5.5 Team Building and Promotion

The question of team building and team leadership is one of the key points of an entrepreneurial digital strategy. Because the times where unique selling points were achieved with packaging, color, lettering, and market promotion are long gone. Establishing yourself as a brand takes more than scratching the promotional surface, more than a glossy image. All that counts today is the willingness of staff to think ahead, to think laterally, and their ability to imagine, for example, how imagination precedes the customer in a digital environment. Now, if you are thinking this is just a job for a nerd with an obsession for data, then you are wrong. Teams continue to thrive on their variety and creative drive, just as Peter Drucker, the management guru, has been preaching for decades. Even in these modern times, I consider this way of thinking authoritative: only when people with differing knowledge and backgrounds work together on one project can ideas merge into an overall picture. You need doers just as much as inventors, doubters, and future thinkers. What is important ultimately is that everyone understands the urgency of digitalization and contributes all their talents and strengths to the process.

The trick to managing in Industry 4.0 is to use the abilities of staff in line with strengths and resources. Then—and this is nothing new—staff will progress digitalization with intrinsic motivation because they are undertaking tasks that, quite simply, they enjoy. Digital transformation will not work without enjoyment. After all, contrary to popular belief, the creators are not the machines, but the people who grasp this process and muster the power of imagination to identify the risk of disruption by others ahead of time—opting either for defense or cooperation.

**Focus: Your Digital Team Strategy**

Before deciding on the tasks involved with introducing and implementing a digital strategy together with your team, ensure the following:

- As a manager, you are part of the value creation process.
- You are responsible for product development.
- You know how your product is created.
- You plan, set up, and operate the sustainable use of plants and machinery.
- You ensure that your employees are trained in occupational safety for these plants and machines.
- You guarantee that the machinery life cycle complies with ISO standard 55,000.
- You are aware that any change is dependent on the speed of your production machinery.
- You know that only flexibly upgradeable and removable production machinery fits in with modern value chain architectures.
- You are prepared to encourage your team's creativity and to establish a culture of understanding for mistakes.
- You know that a digital strategy can only be successfully implemented if staff comprehend the need for change as an opportunity.

## 5.6 Defend or Cooperate

I cannot stress this enough: Unique selling points are a thing of the past. Everything has been invented, everything has been said. There are barely any claims of true novelty in products. Brand loyalty is a passé. Nobody operates in isolation anymore. Nobody is detached from the ideas and influences of others—not even in the field of fine arts.

For a long time, book retailers thought their business model untouchable. They offered what people have been making their own since the invention of cuneiform: books for reading and leisure—and competent advice. Their shelves were filled with stories and knowledge and the customer relied on the judgment of the well-read retailer when asking: "What do you recommend?" The book retailer then shrugged their shoulders, full in the knowledge that they were playing a part in determining the success or failure of an author. The book slipped across the counter on their recommendation. That was until bloggers arrived.

When the blogger scene arrived in the world of literature, Amazon had already conquered the digital book market. For a long time, book store retailers ignored the danger. They did not defend themselves. With the blogger scene cheerfully recommending digital books, the mood began to change. While they continued to doubt that anyone could have a preference for digital books, soon they started to prick up their ears, no longer able to ignore the burgeoning problem. Their sales figures forced them to think again. What bloggers were writing on their website and on social networks was attracting interest—more than recommendations in store. Suddenly one blogger was reaching a variety of customers. Blogs were being shared, liked, and links to online order platforms posted. That made a trip to the book store obsolete in the minds of many readers, since blogger websites featured reviews and recommendations and books could be ordered from your sofa at the click of a button.

Had book retailers and their staff perhaps been able to predict this trend, they would have collected, reviewed, and analyzed data on their customers. Then they would have identified a general desire to save time and gain flexibility. The booker retailer did not seem able to make the link between customer time and store opening hours—and spent many years without any effort to optimize this stage in its value creation process. It stuck to its analog model, maintaining a backward-looking approach, book retailers would not fall prey to the acceleration of networks anyway. Their recommendations, their knowledge, and their customer advice: all untouchable. Customers always penalize entrepreneurial stubbornness. In our example, the customer seeks out about book summaries online on blogger websites. With a glass of red wine and some classical music, the customer flicked through the sections and, to her delight, found order links taking her directly to Amazon, buch.de, and other platforms. A decline in sales and bankruptcies in in-store retail soon followed. It was not until then that the first companies started to recognize that networks and cooperation might be an effective approach. Today even the smallest book store in the furthest flung rural backwater knows: without digital structures, without the cooperation of bloggers, without a web presence and the option of communicating and ordering digitally, the future is anything but bright. The *Börsenblatt des*

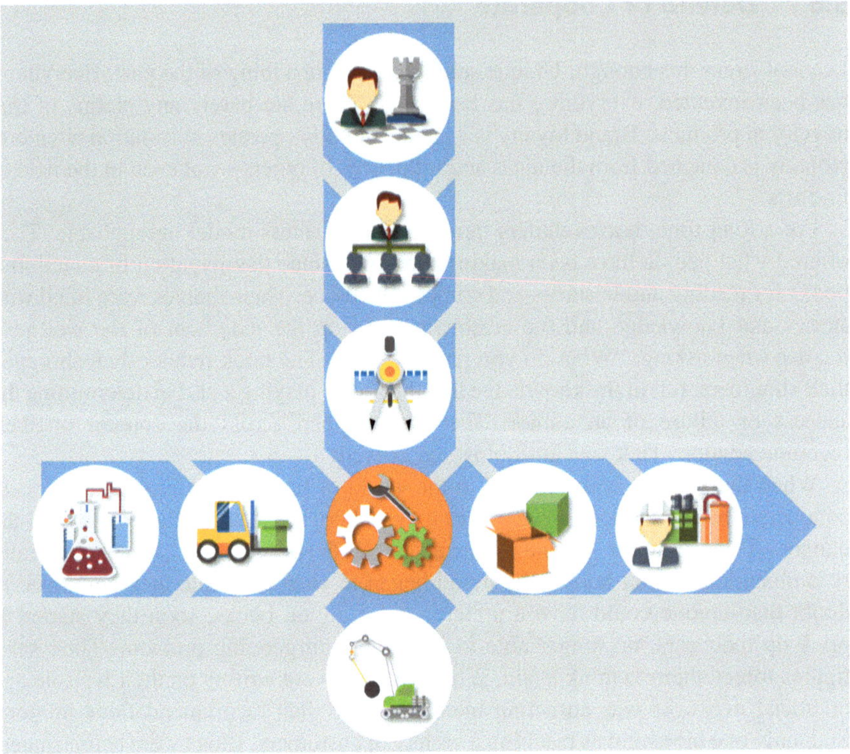

**Fig. 5.1** In-house production as a singular element in a value chain from a company perspective

*Deutschen Buchhandels* (the German book trade gazette) recently reported that: "While the Amazon partner program has been a source of genuine delight for some time now, bloggers are increasingly sending their site visitors links to book stores around the corner (. . .) And so the two groups flirt shyly with one another, mutually attracted to one another, but don't really have any idea of how they should come together away from the digital world" (Gröger 2015). Bloggers, incidentally, can be recommended by book retailers, publishing their personal book ranking in their store windows. Hybrid models can work too—the e-book and the printed book both have markets, justification, and thus fans. When applying this insight to Industry 4.0 it should be noted that although we will not know where the journey will take us, there is nothing to stop us linking up existing modules. We do not need to dream up any grand strategies today, even small steps between the real and virtual world are worthwhile if they contribute to value creation.

The model in Fig. 5.1 is applicable to almost every industry. Simply replace the central symbol of the production plant as appropriate in: manufacturing, the hotel industry, the printing plant, knowledge management, or wherever your core business sector may lie.

The notion of in-house production as a singular element in a value chain stage from a company perspective (see Fig. 5.1) is applicable to a number of sectors. Companies from almost all sectors are faced with the challenge of increasing their focus on the consumer benefit in order to successfully overcome the challenges of digitized societies.

## References

Gröger K (2015) Neue Liebe? Buchhandel und Blogger. https://www.boersenblatt.net/artikel-neue_liebe_951920.html. Accessed 30 Jan 2017

Kim CW, Mauborgne R (2015) Der Blaue Ozean als Strategie. Wie man neue Märkte schafft, wo es keine Konkurrenz gibt. Hanser, Munich

Simon H, Fassnacht M (2008) Preismanagement: Strategie – Analyse – Entscheidung – Umsetzung, 3rd edn. Springer Gabler, Wiesbaden

# 6 Call to Arms for a Change in Corporate Culture

A change in values and culture are central to the digital transformation +++ Why performance indicators from the past are irrelevant +++ Map out future scenarios +++ How to use stress to positive effect +++ Change is a question of personality too +++ Why company hierarchies are disintegrating +++ Mistakes are key to progression +++ The new guiding principles of industry 4.0

A company without a value-oriented culture would be like a sponge—full of holes and bendable to the point of invisibility. It would fail to generate any attention for its products and services. It would lack image. Only by defining and communicating economic, sociocultural, and organizational value factors can companies ensure the effectiveness of their self-image. This applies to both private and professional spheres since values are, after all, the basis of any form of ethics. These ethics are in the midst of change. In fact, they are on the verge of full transformation. You may welcome this, you may not. The fact is: in digitalization, we are encountering a whole different value dimension which I will set out in this chapter—on the one hand, to encourage you to move with the times; on the other hand, to incite you to think creatively. This is a call to arms to anchor corporate culture in Industry 4.0 but with a modern twist.

If values like tradition, reliability, and permanency in partnerships have been a long-standing feature of your basic framework, I urge you to do away with these immediately. Tradition is an outdated term in the digital age. Reliability is being torn to shreds by digital disruption. Permanency is the enemy of adaptability—I will go on to stress this at length in the next chapter—in this age of digitalization it is of vital importance that you train your adaptability until it becomes a corporate strength.

And still, many managers cling to traditional values like the hero in a Shakespeare drama to his star-crossed lover. In the end both die a painful death. While it may be



A. Weber, *Digitalization for Value Creation*, Future of Business and Finance,
https://doi.org/10.1007/978-3-030-36229-4_6

the fate of a hero to stubbornly fight lost battles, and follow any small glimmer of hope for a happy ending, however long the odds may be, such behavior is not part of the role of a manager. Managers need to be able to change perspective and, above all, perpetually willing to experiment. This brings me to the modern values that are lacking in a number of companies. These include progressive thinking, networking along the value chain, appreciation for staff ideas, and empathy for the end customer. Explore what works, do what is possible.

SMEs are, in particular, hold traditional values up like a trophy and hesitate for too long when it comes to transformation. That is a shame. After all, small- and medium-sized companies dispose of the relevant means to adapt a corporate culture to the requirements of the time: adaptable structures, flat hierarchies, enthusiastic and emotionally involved staff. Large corporations, on the other hand, are sluggish, impeded by organizational guidelines, their actions hampered by drawn-out voting processes. It can take years to win over each individual employee to the transformation process because these large companies lack the loyalty and trust enjoyed by family-run businesses. All that remains is for medium-sized companies to seize the opportunities open to them. These companies may then emerge as the winners of the digitalization process.

## 6.1 Key Indicators for the Future

The penchant managers have for clinging to old performance indicators never ceases to amaze me. Measuring success or failure by figures from years gone by is rarely constructive. While joint-stock companies may be obligated under the accounting policy of the third book of the German Commercial Code (HGB) to submit a management report, notes, and the annual financial statements including balance sheet and profit and loss statement, this obligation need not necessarily entail backward thinking. Yet managers are obsessed with these statistics from days gone by, even using them as a means of predicting what is to come.

This is an example of how backward thinking manifests itself in a corporate culture. The past is becoming a crutch to stop companies from stumbling. Statistics and performance indicators are crutches: the same recurring criteria are compared time and time again. Few of the points in product life cycles are taken into consideration. Attempts are made to find excuses and explanations for details and, ultimately, companies talk themselves into failure. They blame the political framework conditions. They claim staff turnover was high. I have even seen urgently needed changes go ignored in the hope of obtaining past performance figures. Worse still: in the German industry we are seeing changes launched as a means of achieving old results on the basis of past figures rather than any attempts to move forward. Managers are going to mammoth efforts to develop strategies to delay the future! Then results are twisted to force them into a specific mold in spite of the fact that we are in an age which requires a completely new mode of thought and action. In this accelerated world, we can no longer afford the luxury of constant reflection, waiting, or mulling over all the options. While this may still be a job for philosophers, the fact remains that this kind of aestheticism has no place in management. Adopting the pose of the Thinker by Rodin, chin balanced on fist, for the sake of brooding and doubting will not get anyone far here. What is required is a spirited courageous approach to the future, even if this entails a certain element of risk.

But this will not work if we simply polish up the old and brand it "new." The macroeconomic situation is damaged by the excuses of managers who have not learned to let go of these crutches and draw a line under dated and obsolete performance indicators. *Think big!* That should be the today's motto to fire industry up for the future.

What would happen

- If we did not look to the past for information?
- If we were to set out our performance indicators for the next 5 years *in advance* and proceed on the basis of the best-case scenario that we could dream of?
- If we were to turn away from the figures of the past and set ourselves greater goals than experience would lead us to expect?

Objectives and imagination are the key ingredients to success. Imagination allows you to visualize what you would have to do to become the best company that you could be. Figures do of course play a role here, but not as significant a role as they have done previously. They are calculated at more frequent intervals and corrected continuously. This can be worked out digitally. With today's analytics tools you can use political, economic, and corporate parameters or assumptions that you make to map out the likelihood of your future growth—regardless of the past. There are simple and easy-to-learn solutions for this (e.g., *Tableau* software) which can help you to come up with scenarios. You can lay out your assumptions virtually and simulate the implications of decisions. These tools are readily available. They do not cost an awful lot but can help you to learn quickly and effectively. And this approach is also far more creative than hopeful performance indicator comparisons. Imagine a model with five setting wheels. One stands for political framework conditions, one for the economic situation, one for your action as a company on the market, one for your staff, and one for your customers. Which one do you turn first to grow? What consequences will emerge in the overall concept? When will your value chain stage require adaptation? Muse away to your heart's content! Let your mind wander, visualizing what is possible, linking data from different silos and learning how to expand or even completely redesign your value chain stage with the information gleaned from this. The individual steps are shown in Fig. 6.1.

The most important learning steps toward optimizing your value chain stage will leave you in no doubt: tradition is no longer a guarantee of success. This is now being replaced by company adaptability and the ability to offer things quickly and in line with consumer expectations.

One characteristic of digitalization is the rapid pace at which fiction and reality are converging. In the initial years following its launch, Facebook recorded only

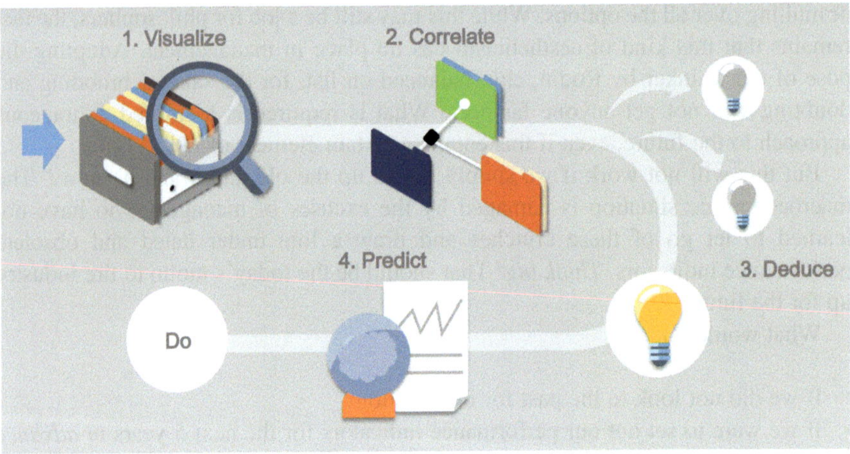


**Fig. 6.1** Learning steps toward optimizing your value chain stage

sluggish growth. No reason not to believe in the idea. Those were probably Mark Zuckerberg's thoughts back in the first few years between 2007 and 2009 when his business model was struggling to gain momentum. And the rest is history: an increase of 50% in one quarter of 2015 compared with the previous year period and prospects of continued success on an astronomical scale. There is a lesson here too: Success is no numbers game. It is emotion, purpose, belief in your own innovative drive, and an endless imagination. While I am not a fan of looking for archetypes in business, success stories like this can serve as motivation to push people out of their comfort zone. Tradition is no longer a guarantee of success. Pack tradition away in a box with all your other memories. Write a book about it for your grandchildren to read. That would be a valuable way of holding on to your past performances.

Then adopt a panorama view, discover new things. Reinvent yourself! Now is your chance to swim away from unwieldy corporations and be the first to reach that deep blue ocean. The trick is to ask yourself, continually and honestly: how can change succeed in the company? By replacing the value of tradition with the value of adaptability. I fear it will still be some time before German companies have internalized this adaptability. While I may be seeing this more and more often in mission statements, this alone will not be enough. After all, the written word becomes an empty platitude if bosses and staff do not live it with joy and optimism. But many managers and staff shy away from this. The reason is a human one: living through change means stress—something we want to avoid by all means necessary. Health consultants go even further and say that stress leads to exhaustion. I think statements like these are dangerous in the age of digitalization. People can be trained to cope with stress, provided an intensive phase is followed by a more relaxed phase and provided stress is rooted in optimism—not fear.

## 6.2 Change Means Stress

Stress occurs as soon as habits change. That is a truth that applies to digitalization too. It applies to everyone, to managers, as well as staff. But I regard stress as a driving force for success, provided it does not exceed a certain duration.

Yes, change can hurt. Imagine that you have been signing your letters and contracts with a special pen for years and years. It sits well in your hand; its quality and form reflect the price. For you this pen is a sort of status symbol—let us say, a special edition Montblanc pen. You associate this pen with your ascension up the career ladder, it symbolizes positive emotions because you bought it with your first manager's salary. It makes you nostalgic for your early days in the job and time rich in opportunity. Now imagine the following. Your line manager has an announcement to make: "From now on all writing in this company will be done with the new logo pen. It has a built-in chip card for registering time and one for the door opener's laser scanner." You look at the pen—and think it looks *spacey* but ugly. You have zero emotional attachment to this clunky item. You bristle, you want to protest, but the resolute look on the face of your superior tells you: "No buts!" We have invested in new technology, and we are going to use it. Change always involves stress. How high the pressure gage rises depends on the respective personal level of internal objection. The same applies to the introduction of new technologies, workflows, perspectives, and company values.

The more resistance a staff member displays, the harder it is for change to succeed. The Baby Boomer generation, in particular, invariably measures up anything new against its own experiences before going any further. That in itself prompts skepticism and that maybe one of the reasons why this particular generation clings to symbols and often maintain a backward way of thinking. Generation Y employees tick differently. They are curious, they were brought up with innovative technologies. They think in results and that makes them open to change. The focus is no longer on grand objectives but rather on the outcome and the question: am I on the right path or do I need to alter my course? Therefore, I recommend that you estimate the likely resistance to any change and take a sensitive approach, particularly to opponents. People move to their own distinct rhythms. Taking note of this can minimize stress.

## 6.3 Enduring Small Indignities

Dissatisfaction should not be allowed to develop into misery over an extended period. This leaves managers preoccupied with getting their team back on track instead of working together to answer the all-important question: "Where do we see our next challenge?" That is why it is important to take the concerns of each individual staff member seriously, before quickly making it clear to him or her that the company has no option other than to implement this transformation process. The dialog is important. Prior clarification is indispensable. If, however, an employee continues to abstain from commitment to the change process, the consequences of this should be clearly stated. In other words: a break from the company. Adaptability is a value firmly anchored in modern corporate culture. Corporations have taken this on board and so must staff, acting appropriately in the process.

Large corporations generally undergo a change process every 3–4 years. To make this run smoothly, many have introduced a job rotation principle. In other words: every 5 years staff members must leave their job, team, and department and turn their attentions to new tasks. The idea behind this is, first of all, to counter inflexibility and stubborn attitudes. Secondly, studies have shown that staff fall into routine mode after 5 years. They work to a limited performance standard and are no longer passionate about their tasks. My recommendation to small- and medium-sized companies would be to anchor this flexibility in your business culture in preparation for the ongoing change process set in motion by digitalization.

Personal sensitivities should not feature in this. I myself once found myself in a situation of uncertainty. My line manager, with whom I had a good working relationship and a history of project success, was assigned to a new task area. I harbored a few reservations as to whether I would be able to work as effectively with his successor. If felt it deep in the pit of my stomach, and I perceived this as an inner resistance to this change. What I was feeling was the limits of my own adaptability. It took a while until I could admit that to myself. Yet the process was important for me and my development. Personal further development is a process that is never devoid of emotion. Small reservations can be advantageous in the era of digitalization too, certainly better than forging ahead as if blinkered. In times of change, it is important every now and then to change perspective and say to yourself: "It's not about friendship. It's about business success, and today that means optimizing value chain stages." We must leave our reservations behind us, even if a few personal bruises remain. Otherwise you risk disruption to your own business model by others—and pain far worse.

## 6.4 A Question of Personality

As soon as uncertainty arises in relation to roles and jobs, the neural mix accumulates stress hormones in the blink of an eye. Not everyone has the personality structure to cope with change easily. There are even people who view change as a threat to their existence. Refuting such fantasies is one of the key tasks of modern management. When people ask me how negative emotions such as anger and irritation can be converted into positive emotions such as surprise and joy, I quote Antoine de Saint-Exupéry: "If you want to build a ship, don't drum up people to collect wood and don't assign them tasks and work, but rather teach them to long for the endless immensity of the sea."

Consultants like Fredmund Malik refer to this management approach as a "contribution to the whole." In his bestseller "*Führen. Leisten. Leben,*" he uses an anecdote about three bricklayers to illustrate this point: a passerby watches them work for a while, before asking the first one: "What are you doing there?" The man answers with sad, tired eyes: “I’m trying to earn a living.” The passerby nods and turns to the second bricklayer with the same question. His eyes are brighter, and he sounds proud when he responds: “I am the best bricklayer in all the land.” Impressed, the passerby lingers a while to watch the skilled craftsman before asking the third man: “And what are you doing?” He looks up and looks at the passerby thoughtfully. He looks at his work and then off into the distance. He lets his thoughts drift off and suddenly a glimmer appears in his eyes: “I am helping to build a cathedral ...” (Malik 2013).

You guessed it, the last bricklayer will work through his stress quicker, he will not lose sight of the bigger picture in the midst of change. That is because he regards himself as a participant—and not a victim.

**Focus: Your Change Management**

As soon as your staff recognize the part they play in the value chain stage and, furthermore, the value chain as a whole, they will develop an intrinsic sense of contribution, ideally this will grow into enthusiasm. But this takes time. As such, my advice to you would be: make it clear that change is not generally a smooth process and that it can falter again and again. Aggrieved staff will reject the new situation and try desperately to cling to old traditions wherever possible. Only once this has been overcome will they come to a realization, ideally developing into identification with the changed structures. From this point, your job is to achieve the ideal emotion curve (see Fig. 6.2). Such resistance can actually be “deprogrammed” or vice versa: adaptability trained!

Staff view change processes as shocking events with a negative impact on motivation. The rationale and purpose behind the changes are rejected. Only at the lowest point of the curve comes the realization: Change is coming, nobody can stop it. Only then will staff accept the argument. They look at the potential advantages and start to create, provided they can see the benefit. The identification phase sees staff become participants and begin to motivate others. There is an overcompensation with regard to motivation. The potentially attainable level grows far in excess of the original level. The whole process—from shock to identification—will tie up a great deal of the company’s capacity. Thus, the aim should be to level off the momentum of the curve by means of targeted training and transparent communication of objectives and requirements.

## 6.5 The Collapse of the Pyramid

To summarize, corporate cultures in Industry 4.0 are characterized by multicultural, tolerant, hierarchy-busting, trust-based, and forgiving values. In just a few more years progressive companies will no longer have any pyramidal structures, acting like a boss will be a thing of the past, given the risk this would pose to optimizing the

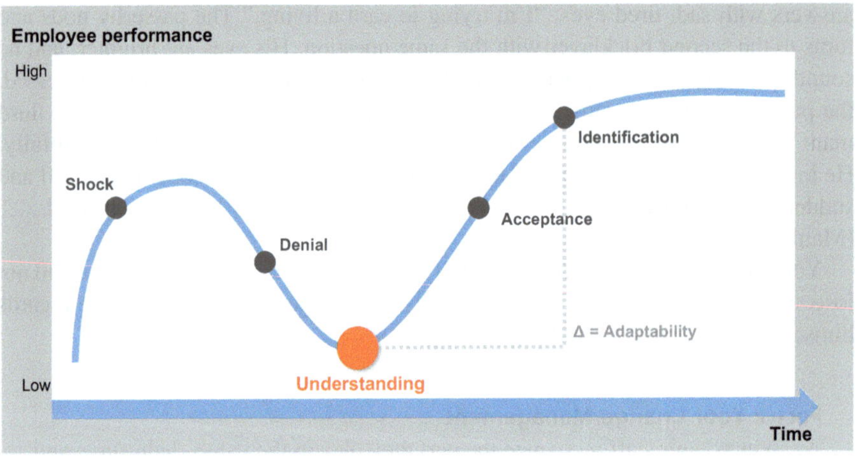


**Fig. 6.2** Progression of emotional staff reactions in the change process

value chain stage. This means corporate culture will no longer be "decreed" from the top-down—ultimately it will be shaped where it functions every day, within the remit of each individual employee. Hardly anyone without an active social media presence has their finger on the pulse. In your role as a manager, you must gather information and ideas from all your staff. Use them to better recognize customer requirements and to drive the digital transformation process forward.

Swarm behavior means:

- Drawing a picture of your own value creation as a constituent part of the entire chain right through to the end customer benefit.
- Continually refining this picture and considering your own specific business needs in the value chain stage and incorporating these in the overall value chain.

I view swarming behavior as something which is firmly anchored in changing corporate cultures, and this term should not be confused with swarm intelligence here. The former means involving employees and, furthermore, the peripheral players in the value chain stage, in order to find solutions for the future which are both appropriate and viable. The latter involves individual opinions being suppressed in the interests of collectivity—something I regard as dangerous. So, let us remain on the subject of swarm behavior, used for many years by BMW, which set up a so-called "co-creation lab" and asked its customers to submit technology, design, and driving ideas. A move that is both exemplary and very smart, providing management with first-hand access to valuable suggestions. Does the end customer explain their requirements—what better way for a company to look into the future? It astounds me how hesitant other companies are to respond to this and use this success

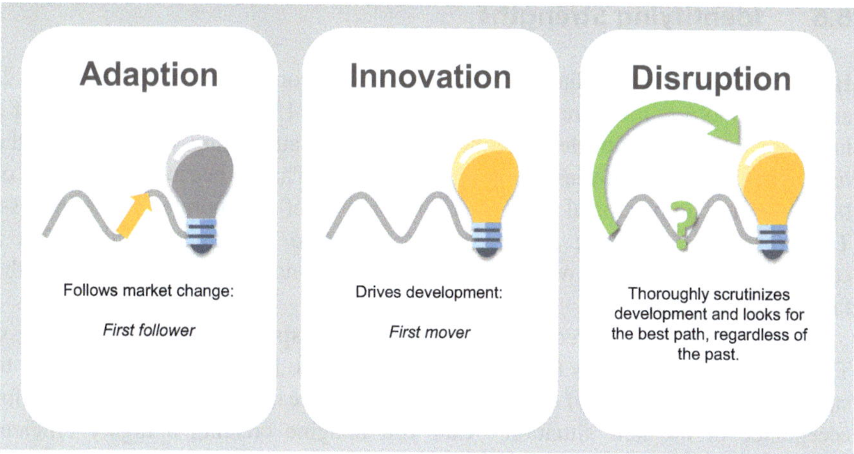


**Fig. 6.3** Change level cascade

model themselves. This is, after all, an opportunity to collect data, analyze information, and maintain contacts. I would urge you to make use of these ideas:

- Use the contacts, information, and ideas of your employees.
- Transfer responsibility for success to your staff.
- Encourage them to say their thoughts aloud and take these suggestions seriously.
- Communicate with your customers about your products.
- Involve the customer in your value creation stage and instill in them an emotional stake in your corporate culture.

**Focus: The Three Levels of Development Possibilities**

Encourage your staff to use social media both privately and professionally and to analyze it in the interests of the company. A modern corporate culture requires a combination of business and leisure. The employee sees themselves as a mediator between the product and the customer and knows the part they play in the value chain stage. The model in Fig. 6.3 serves to illustrate the new cascade of employee emotions and to identify the three levels of development options. Adaptations to existing solutions are a low-risk means of coming up with new products without the development and innovation costs. Here there is the risk that these will be replaced by highly dynamic market changes. Innovative companies anticipate change and further develop products—risking failure in the process. At the same time these companies are prime candidates for the transformation of value chains because change already forms part of the company's DNA. Disruptive companies look for radical solutions without considering any potential destruction of existing value chains. They are risk-seeking—with the strength and courage to forge new paths. Their actions are guided by solutions. These companies usually pursue ideas that accurately reflect the consumer benefit.

## 6.6 Identifying Strengths

How long employees remain at the denial stage of a corporate change (see Fig. 6.2) and which motives there are for doing so is a subject I have been working on for a long time. I have conducted countless interviews, attempting to investigate the reasons for some employees' refusal to be moved. That is because knowledge of these reasons can be crucial to the success or failure of a corporate change process. Too protracted a learning process means decreased performance and almost a complete standstill for innovation. This is something no company can afford in the fast-paced digital age.

The aim should be to predict staff reactions and to speed up the learning process. The provocation method is the tried and tested choice for this. It uses questions to stimulate the imagination of employees and aims to create a stimulus in the brain for acceptance of the new situation: "Can you imagine creating a highly efficient opportunity for analyzing customer data and responding to their needs almost in real-time by merging IT and Engineering departments? What role can you play in helping to achieve this? Have a think about this and report back to me tomorrow. I look forward to hearing your ideas." What on the surface seems emotionally motivated remains nothing more than rhetoric that serves the company's own interests, i.e., lifting the employee to the next stage of the ideal line. As you may have guessed, I am advocating another method, one that centers around the employee and their desire to play a part: I look for talent in the employee. I find out where their strengths lie by asking questions, talking, and observing. Often this is reflected in their hobbies. Does the employee exhibit musical talent or play chess, is he or she actively involved in politics or youth work? I know that this is exactly where their enthusiasm finds expression, that this is exactly where they can drive the company forward with their physical, mental, and emotional ability.

An employee who can use his strengths and constantly fine grinding, the urge continues, who wants to exceed his personal limits. He does not stay in his comfort zone. That is exactly what is needed in the digital age: to throw the shutters wide open and to look far beyond your own value chain stage. Thoughts and actions will no longer be confined within company borders in the future. These are dissolving. They are merging with the overall value chain of which your company/your department/you yourself only represents one stage. If you want to continue to optimize this stage, then you need to recognize where you need to raise your game, your value, as well as your contribution to the benefit of the end customer. We need curious employees, driven by a desire for progress. Have a close look at who fits each role given their strengths. Then give this employee the freedom to organize their own tasks and structure processes within their remit. This will result in a twofold improvement:

1. The personal satisfaction of the employee. Nothing is more fulfilling than harnessing your own strengths.
2. The adaptability of your company. Given the chance to exploit their potential on a daily basis, employees will want to go on and on. It pushes them forward to undergoing further training and gaining new insights.

This does of course involve an element of risk: Such employees maybe even more ambitious than you. This may lead them not only identifying potential attacks on your value chain stage but questioning the entire company. Unfortunately, some managers do not appreciate the value of such doubts, which come as a result of the wonderful ability to think ahead and outside of the box. They view this doubt instead as disloyalty. Ideally this employee would be applauded, praised for their outstanding service, for their future vision. Because you can be sure that there are threats to your company that are not obvious. It would be good if you had the capability, thanks to a strength-centered, open, corporate culture, to predict and identify these yourself before the threat became existential. Clinging to compliance rules is associated with an inability to let thoughts roam and serves only to stifle curiosity.

Encourage your staff to break with tradition—and above all, to contradict you as a manager! Even university professors face constant critique from their students in their lectures and seminars. Namely when they Google information in real time that they can use to question the arguments of the professor. It is amazing how processes can come alive with this kind of communication! How detailed the criticism and improvement of a process can be! And how wonderfully true the words of a great philosopher still ring. So much so that they could easily pass as a slogan for modern corporate culture despite being about 2400 years old:

"I know that I know nothing (Socrates)."

**Focus: Accelerated Change Momentum**

The better you can identify the strengths of your employees, the more stress free the change phase (see Fig. 6.4) will be. An employee who can use their professional and personal strengths at work will go the extra mile when it comes to contributing their knowledge and emotion to the process. They will be intrinsically motivated to successfully shape the change process and to involve themselves in this process with their own physical, mental, and emotional abilities. The transition from the change phase to the consolidation phase should take place as quickly as possible with a view to then bringing about further change and consolidation. In contrast to classic change management, whereby every change process is followed by a training and stabilization phase, the speed of the waves of change in digitized value chains hardly allows any acclimatization time. Consolidation phases are completely swallowed up by perpetual optimization measures. Companies and employees must learn that change is not a threat but an opportunity. As well as a changed management approach, there is a need to allow freedoms with regard to developments and error culture.

The transformation of value chains is subject to a momentum that is picking up speed. Structures are changing faster, companies are being divided up, sold, acquired, disappearing from value chains completely, being replaced, etc. This is leading to an ever-quickening rate of change and an ever-shortening of the consolidation or "practice" phase following change.

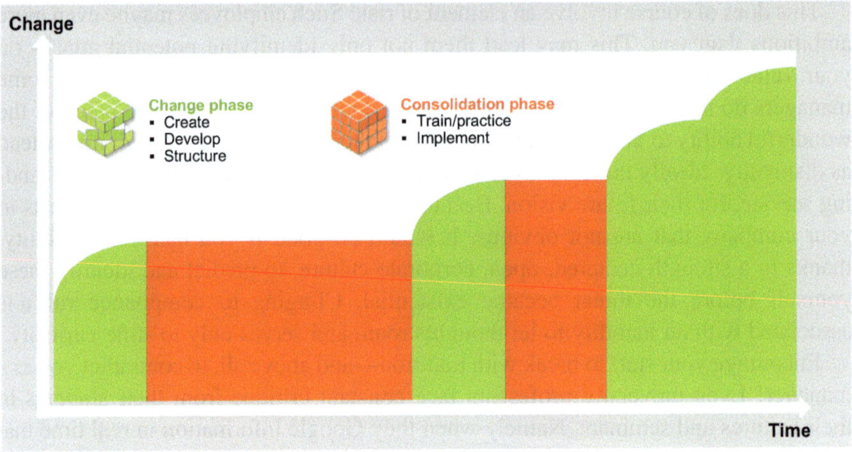


**Fig. 6.4** Model of change dynamic in fast-developing companies

## 6.7 Recognizing the Value in Mistakes

The corporate culture required by digitalization does not rule out employee mistakes. Quite the opposite in fact. It encourages employees to do exactly that, to make mistakes, to talk about them and to involve others in flawed processes and to let them in on the insight acquired from these. Employees should no longer have to ask with hanging shoulders to speak with the boss privately, hoping they get away with no more than a warning—and not a firing.

I cannot stress it enough in this book: nobody knows where companies, let alone entire sectors are going. Anything is possible in the digital era because everything is in a constant state of flux. Digitalization is characterized by volatility, uncertainty, complexity, and ambiguity.

An entire value chain can collapse if one single company does not abide by the rules of transparent communication, focusing on its own key figures instead of the end customer. That change goes hand in hand with the new and unexpected, and that time-honored concepts no longer apply is only natural here. Companies can see all their past experiences become irrelevant in the blink of an eye. The only solution is to be brave, give new things a try and seek out the right tools and mindset. Mistakes will be made in the process. And these mistakes will act as benchmarks for any future strategy. They form the basis of any development. This was discovered back in 1930s by IBM boss Tom Watson. When he noticed that one of his management staff was producing 100,000 Dollar mistakes, he did not waste any time in summoning this man to his office. The employee looked down at his feet. He mumbled an apology and offered to hand in his notice there and then since his mistakes had led to disaster for the company and that the damage caused was inexcusable. Tom Watson listened to his stammering before exclaiming: "Sacked? Why would I sack you? I've just invested 100,000 Dollars in your further training."

There must be a place for mistakes in corporate culture. They must form a part of our mission statement, with a clear statement: mistakes are encouraged. Only by doing so can we ensure innovation does not become a fear-ridden obstacle. By using this statement, you can arouse curiosity for progress, challenging your staff to think ahead—right down the line to the end customer. In doing so you will boost the self-confidence of individual employees. They will take courage in the knowledge that they can rely on this statement when they falter. They can get up again, analyze the mistake with their boss and their team and continue with their tasks. Industry 4.0 is also about analyzing mistakes and adding them to your entrepreneurial experience. If mission statements are written to boost self-perception internally and corporate image externally, then the degree of openness to errors should increase with the degree of progress.

## 6.8 New Guiding Principles in Industry 4.0

When traditions and pyramidal structures become relics, you must ask yourself the question: What are the values that matter today and what are the values that will matter in the future? The following overview is intended to provide you with suggestions, full in the knowledge that you will add to these with the characteristics of your corporate personality:

1. Collaboration

   Sharing, networking, and participation: These values reflect the digital zeitgeist. Do not just integrate your staff in production processes, extend the line to include partners, suppliers, upstream, and downstream companies right through to the end customer.
2. Free spirit

   Jean-Jacques Rousseau once said: "I prefer liberty with danger than peace with slavery." Managers should take the time to digest this. These words serve as a warning against turning staff into puppets, instead encouraging curiosity and a thirst for adventure in teams.
3. Flexibility

   An open-minded approach to developments helps ensure that no theoretical models are excluded. This even includes the possibility of pulling open desk drawers to see what visionary employees have come up with years before. Maybe now is the time to return to these projects, refine them and incorporate them into your company's strategy? Many companies forget to have a look back at past ideas. In the meantime, the environment has changed so much that ideas from long before may now turn out to be the perfect fit.
4. Adaptability

   Be prepared to continually reinvent yourself. Train for change together with your staff before stress has the chance to occur during the change management process. Nobody should have a life-long entitlement to one specific activity. Never tire of dreaming up little changes in processes. This will keep you mentally and emotionally prepared: (1) because the more you practice, the lesser stress becomes, (2) because it trains adaptability, and (3) it improves your ability to adapt to external change.

5. Self-efficacy

   Self-efficacy is used here—in contrast to how it is generally understood—in the sense of constantly questioning whether the environment in which you operate is still the right one. The commitments and contracts that you enter into today can harm you tomorrow. You must be prepared to exit even the most long-standing relationships if this is in the interests of your self-efficacy. Digitalization means moving away from business relationships wherever this is in the interests of your own business model or own transformation process.
6. A forgiving attitude to mistakes

   Take joy in mistakes. The insights gained from these could secure you a decisive edge on the market.
7. Strength orientation

   Allocate tasks within your team according to staff talents. Take note: to encourage talent is to train it with hard work and discipline. Do not forget that even doubters can make a valuable contribution to the team when they are not being obstructive at least. Create a framework for different perspectives and ideas. Use the strengths of your staff to exploit the business potential.
8. Network communication

   Classic organigram structures belong in the past. Today communication takes place without hierarchical barriers. Quite the opposite in fact. It extends right to the periphery of your value chain stage and, on data analysis, right through to the end customer.
9. Trust

   Transformation requires trust, otherwise it would be struck down by doubt. Establish optimism in your company, that is a key indicator of the internal climate and success.
10. Credibility

    Be wary of promising too much, too soon. Only make promises that you can fulfill here and now. Do not disclose what has not yet been underpinned by fact.

## Reference

Malik F (2013) Führen Leisten Leben. Wirksames Management für eine neue Zeit. Campus, Frankfurt am Main, p 98

# Progressive Thinking 7

Put your business model to the test +++ How to make your customers happy +++ The magic power of technology +++ Take staff feelings seriously +++ How open thinking and visualization can help enhance your value creation +++

The good news in this chapter is that politicians are making every effort to push forward digital transformation in German companies. The other news is a little more somber: people are worried about their future. While they relish the onset of the digital revolution in their private lives, they fear the transformation to come in their professional environment. But let us first concentrate on the good news.

Do you remember the uproar that came from the political benches in the German parliament when entrepreneurs called for more freedom of information? Companies wanted to collect and analyze data for use in their in-house production optimization analyses and customer communications. Both corporations and SMEs alike had both recognized that sooner or later they would be left behind by the American and Asian markets if they did not make use of the data they were collecting. So, they called for a more open approach to handling data. But the politicians shook their heads—the objection was that customers' data sovereignty would be put at risk. The tone could not be more different today. Now the issue has become a top-level matter: The Chancellery issued a press release during the 2016 National IT Summit in Saarbrücken: "The principle of data economy can no longer be the general protocol for the development of new products." Angela Merkel herself made it clear: "Politics cannot make data protection rules so restrictive that they render big data management impossible (...) Germany is in possession of a good baseline as regards digitalization, but lags far behind the world leaders" (The German Chancellor 2016).

This note will encourage companies to take a more liberal approach to data and to use it with a view to facilitating scalability and multi-distributor roles. The aim is not simply to lock data away but to anchor the monetization of data (alongside the



A. Weber, *Digitalization for Value Creation*, Future of Business and Finance,
https://doi.org/10.1007/978-3-030-36229-4_7

manufacture of products) as a corporate objective. Both are business models of the future.

**Focus: Achieving Scalability**
You can make your business model scalable by

- Adapting to the changed value chain.
- Considering how you can improve your products and increase the customer benefit.
- Imagining based on scenarios how you can quickly raise and reduce quantities.
- And how you can better anchor yourself in the value chain using data, trusting that you can optimize your resources with additional software and data links in order to grow both vertically and horizontally.

You do not need any elaborate technologies to make your business model scalable—the Internet should suffice to extend your agitation radius. Once there was only one toy retailer who sold goods in a village. It had a monopoly in the sector in its region. Children pressed their noses up against the store window just to get a look at the miniature railway set. Mothers bought Christmas and birthday gifts there, the retailer was their go-to supplier for many years. Now a new anonymous online retailer is offering its goods, e.g., train sets, dolls, arts, and crafts materials, etc.—and doing so on a larger scale. It draws in the customers from the village online, and it will sell its goods anywhere else in the world too. Looking a little further down the line: the small store on the corner has transformed from a brick-and-mortar store into an online retailer and is on its way to becoming a completely invisible company in the depths of the Internet. It looks instead for distribution partners on other continents who will take care of sales on its behalf.

The former store owner is integrating himself in a value chain, and he is willing to forgo his name in favor of a new business model. For him it is merely a question of product sales—not an image. The "Made in Germany" label is no longer relevant, especially in the eyes of the younger generation. They want to see a customer benefit—not the quality seal. They go online and order what their friends have recommended to them on social networks. Brand loyalty is a value that is no longer relevant, long since having been replaced by online communication. Company marketing departments will have to come to terms with this too. After all, there are new standards in advertising too. Review portals, tweets, posts, and even automatically controlled social bots influence customer behavior. Opinions are formed online.

Amazon is servicing this development par excellence. A customer needs a washing machine, orders it from the Internet giant, and has little interest in whether this washing machine came from Media-Saturn's warehouse stock or an electronics store in Leipzig. All that matters to the customer is that the price is right and that the delivery happens straight away. These kinds of multichannel platforms regulate demand and do not rely on person-to-person customer communication. The aim of this is to use data to determine customer requirements and emphasize benefits. If we continue to spin this web of the future economy, only non-channel platforms will supply customers, and every single process along the digital value chain, from raw materials purchasing right through to logistics, will take place on an automated basis. Customers express their needs both verbally and non-verbally, and value chains optimize themselves accordingly. Then quantities are defined and the result optimized.

Data is already supplying a very accurate picture of what demand is occurring and when. There are very good models of user behavior (at IBM and Microsoft, for example). This is enabling companies to tap into even broader distribution channels and has seen them opt for the diversification business model.

Development in e-commerce (see Fig. 7.1) is driven by increased customer satisfaction. In phase 5 sales channels are waning in significance. In an attempt to create comprehensive customer experiences, customer processes are merging with customer communications.

This change in e-commerce behavior is driven not least by a change in technology, from what started out as no more than an online business card to a complex demand-controlled value creation.

Up until recently it was hard to imagine that a detergent manufacturer could equally offer batteries, tools, and stockings. The customer would have been irritated by these product differences. This is now a possibility given the multi-networks in existence today. On the one hand, any company can relabel its products to penetrate new markets. On the other hand, multi-networks can help it to market a product, let us say a flame cutting machine, in various different sectors. All it needs to do is neutralize, digitize, balance, and adapt its products. This is no longer the stuff of future dreams, it is available, it just needs to be used.

There are of course risks associated with running your business on a solely digital basis.

A hacker might override your security mechanisms tomorrow, you might sustain major damages as a result of malicious online manipulation. But, equally, your warehouse building could burn down, or a manager could disclose the corporate information to your competitors. Maybe there will be an attack, maybe not. Life is not without its risks, online, or offline. That is why I do not like to deal in absolutes. You will always find a hundred different reasons why the time is not right, be it a lack of money, a lack of adequately trained staff, etc. before you start. Here I would advise that you take a systematic approach. Yes, spend a brief time assessing the potential risks, let us say, for 30 min. Then leave pessimism behind. Turn around, roll up your sleeves and summon your team: "Time to move forward. Time for us to shape the future. Otherwise someone else will do it for us—and that is something we cannot allow to happen." This mindset would make your life a great deal easier.

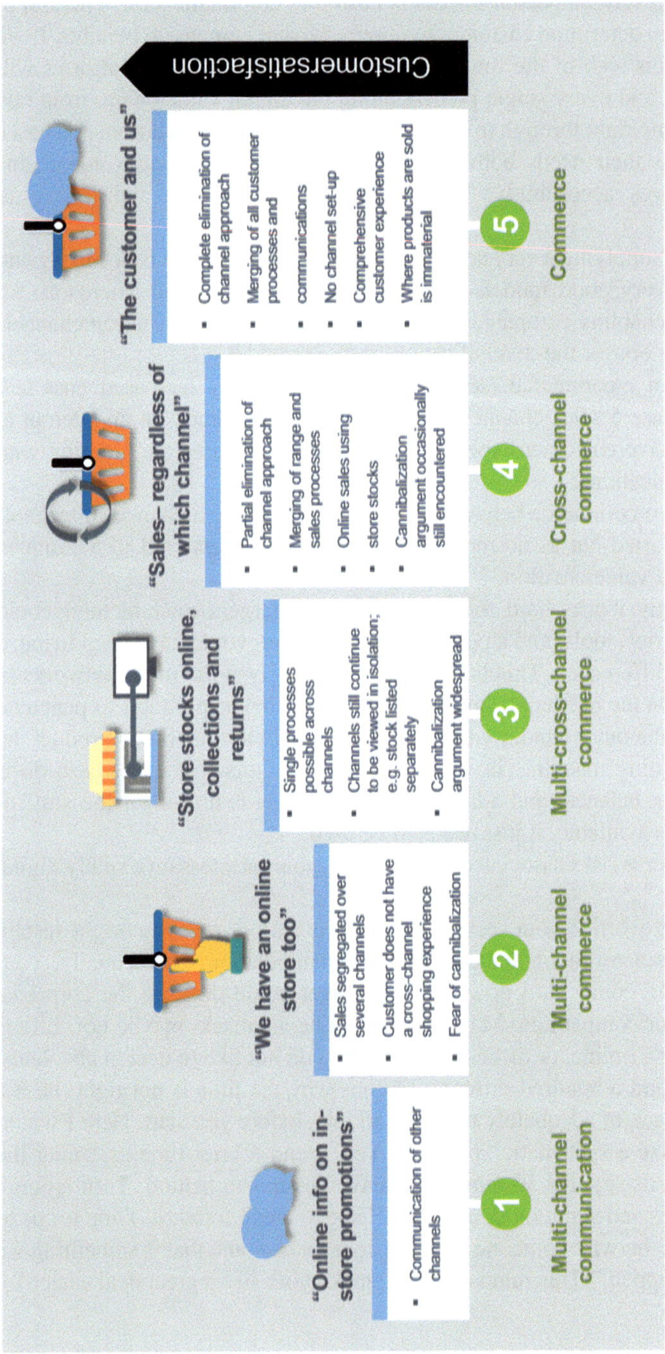


**Fig. 7.1** E-Commerce transformation over time

## 7.1 A Kind of Happiness

Being able to store new things in your mind as ever-available knowledge requires a learning and training phase. And it is down to us to give this new information a positive or negative slant. After ordering a canvas painting online and pressing the "deliver now" button, I waited excitedly to see if the delivery service would really ring the doorbell an hour later. According to the online confirmation, the delivery was to take place at 17:57. At 17:55 a man did indeed appear at the door with the picture. "Amazing!" I thought it does not get much more convenient than that and turned to confirm receipt. "We have to wait two minutes," stammered the delivery man. "The system hasn't released the picture." A minor glitch that causes nothing more than slight amusement. After all, the bottom line is that I saved at least 3 h of my life. I was not stuck in traffic or in the queue for the counter. Saving time is a special kind of happiness.

If you were to ask me whether digitalization makes people happy, I would be, no not entirely. Happiness is, after all, always a snapshot and, above all, comes down to the individual. But one thing that is certain is that part of your happiness depends on your financial security. In order to preserve this part, you as a manager or employee will not able to shut yourself off to digitalization. You will have to think further ahead than previously to secure your job. Further training will be unavoidable. You will have to be optimistic and courageous. There are no boundaries, no walls, and no doors anymore. You should be creative, agile, curious, and global: all traits that characterize happy people.

But still people worry—and this takes me to the second message of this chapter.

## 7.2 Technology Is Like Magic

People worry. They worry about their health, world peace, and their kids' school grades. They worry about whether their partner loves them, sometimes their bank account, their career, and their future, of course. That is fine up to a certain point, because worry is a part of empathy which differentiates humans from robots. Care should be taken, however, to ensure that this does not become the central focus of your thinking. At the moment fears and worry are being stoked primarily by psychologists who are warning that digitalization can make people ill. According to them, it is forcing people to multitask which is against their neurobiological nature. They feel that it dictates 24/7 availability and leads to increasingly more complex tasks and that it will soon lead to humans being replaced by machines. I find this kind of posturing to be damaging. It puts people under stress. It casts an ominous show over the future and shoots down any optimism for an exciting new era before it has even started.

Digitalization must not become a cause for concern, that would only serve to obstruct our view of the opportunities arising from it. But yet this seems to be *en vogue*. That is why the online magazine *Edge* interviewed the smartest minds on the earth on what keeps them awake at night (egde.org 2016). This included the reflections of scientists, philosophers, and writers. One answer, in particular, concerned me. It came from the physicist Neil Gershenfeld and will no doubt become an aphorism. What plagues him is the worry that we are starting to treat technology like magic. I find this statement fascinating. But I want to give it a positive slant. I think this magic spark should catch on in every company, it should instill digital creativity in even the last 20% of hesitators in the German industry. It should become a universally accepted mission statement: "Technology is like magic." A phrase to generate optimism and excitement for the future. We would finally change perspectives—out with worry and in with creativity. We could start to shape the transformation process. While we should of course approach any change with the due vigilance, we must not do so without optimism that the future holds more opportunities than disasters. If the German industry starts to lay the groundwork now it can take German citizens to the forefront of global business and achieve more prosperity than they had ever hoped for.

"The intelligent networking of people, machines and industrial processes is regarded as one of today's most far-reaching changes in the manufacturing industry and in associated economic sectors such as logistics. The Cyber Security Report (Deutsche Telekom/T-Systems 2015), published annually by Telekom, states that 'following the invention of the steam engine, mass production assisted by conveyor belts and electricity and the use of electronics and IT for increased automation in production the term 'industry 4.0' should indicate the scale of this change." Grasping the scale is far more useful than going along with the fears of critics. It is time for German companies to take a leading role on the international level. I would like to put the onus here on managers and call on their creative drive. Lose the philosophical attitude and become a role model for your team. Be optimistic about the future and, above all: ignore your doubts—they are often nothing more than pseudo legitimation for a lack of courage.

## 7.3 Not Without Emotions

Digitalization requires a high degree of adaptability on the part of you and your staff. It is exactly this which gives it an unpredictable character: 80% of which is emotion and 20% of which is rationality. We know from a number of different surveys that around three quarters of all large- to medium-sized companies have drawn up a digital strategy to define objectives and lay down measures. These feature detailed descriptions of how data security is to be established, how data is used, and the programs which will be used for automatic processes. They are legally and technically watertight in the best sense of the word. But again, and again we are hearing that such strategies lose their clout as soon as staff begin to a skeptical view of the change. In a word: the German industry has made preparations for this change—only as of yet, they have failed to take into account the soft factors, such as emotion, in their calculations.

Adaptability is not simply a question of clicking your fingers. It is an ongoing emotional hygiene task. To me there is little sense in a boss banging his fist on the table and pushing an item onto the agenda with a gung-ho approach: "If we do not achieve this goal, heads are going to roll. If you do not create more transparency and share your data, then you will effectively be blocking our communications. This will lead directly to bankruptcy." Threats like this create resistance among staff and, in the event of doubt, may cause them to pick up the phone and call the headhunter.

It is therefore clear that the pace at which a company can progress is more to do with staff mood than strategy. The more you encourage them to learn and make mistakes, the better the mood in the team will be. Organizations must learn this mindset. They have time! The digital transformation is after all still a long way from reaching its peak. There is a lot of unchartered territory ahead of us. We can still decide where we want to make our mark and the obstacles we should avoid. The trick of modern management will be sparking staff enthusiasm for the adventure ahead. That is a matter of priority. This will require intuition, appreciative communication, and positive psychology.

Incidentally, by intuition, I mean not expecting the same reaction from all staff. In a time where there is a greater division between the generations than ever before with regard to the way they communicate and behave, older employees can easily be left feeling unsettled. The Baby Boomers in your team still exhibit strengths such as commitment and patience—while your digital natives primarily think in terms of short projects. At first glance the latter may perhaps seem like the preferable option. After all, the transformation process should have a better chance of success with young people with an affinity for all things digital. No, it will not. Restricting your team to a purely technological focus may sacrifice your link to the end customer. We need people with a high degree of empathy as well as those who are born inventors. Yes, we even need doubters who stop for a minute and ask: are we doing this properly? Only those who are capable of questioning themselves on a daily basis can prevent disruption by third parties. Future-proof teams require input from a range of personalities: creative minds, the hesitant, sticklers for detail, doers, and hands-on project types. Each one has their own temperament, their own potential. So, hear my plea: be patient with your older staff, take their worries about the future seriously. Stop and ask yourself how an employee would feel if they had been stuck in an analog working routine for the last 20 or 30 years. They know their tasks by heart They have appropriated a deep understanding of each individual working step, routine synapses have formed in their minds because they have done the same thing every day for as long as they can remember. As of yet there are no means of breaking down these synapses overnight and rewiring these. That requires time and light-hearted openness. However, in my mind, there is little room for dwelling on these doubts for too long. Listen to the objections of any of your employees who may be harboring any doubts. Thirty minutes. No longer. Then turn your attentions to the future and scope out all the potential opportunities digitalization has to offer.

## 7.4 Sidesteps Welcome

I have given this chapter the title "Progressive thinking"—and by that, I do not mean some kind of fanciful journey in thought. What I mean is a willingness to take a step back before you continue. This may seem paradoxical, but in fact, it is logical. Imagine you were to adopt a witty Socrates quote as a motto for half an hour each day. The Greek thinker made it his business to question everything. He took nothing, absolutely nothing, at face value. In his mind success was no more than a superficial gloss in life. Deep beneath that hid the significant truths that he wanted to elicit. Hence his quote: "I know that I know nothing." The wisest person of his time questioned everything he knew to equip himself for new solutions every day.

I find it remarkable how this Socratic quote has retained relevance all the way into the digital era. It can even become a method if you and your team use this mental trick to analyze and optimize your value chain stage and see adaptability as a continuous task.

This approach, incidentally, is by used Greenpeace too. Even this modern organization frequently dreams up scenarios under the slogan of ignorance. They ask themselves: What would happen if the most intelligent person on the face of the earth were to join us tomorrow? What would they think of our project and what improvements would occur to them? What would happen if we did not know anything about our model and had the chance to rebuild it with an archetypal architecture?

Leave well-worn tracks behind, reflect on your business from a different perspective, as if you were to reset all your previous achievements at the touch of a button. Reset. A white paper for a fresh new plan. Anything is possible. You rewind the chain of adaption (followers), innovation (first movers), disruption (disrupters) again (see. Fig. 6.3). You pose the following question to the team:

1. Is what we are doing for the market still relevant?
2. Why are we doing, what we are doing today, and who is it benefiting?
3. Have the regulations and guidelines on the basis of which we work changed?
4. Has the market in which we operate changed?
5. What can we do better knowing what we currently know?
6. Which technologies can boost our performance?
7. How can we research where we will be useful?
8. How can we identify which role we play in the overall value chain?
9. Who can advise us whether this value chain stage is useful and valuable to others?
10. How can we make processes more transparent and how can we network and utilize data?
11. How can we document results and supply them to others in the company?
12. Where should we invest, where should be saved, and how can we establish ongoing evaluation in the company?

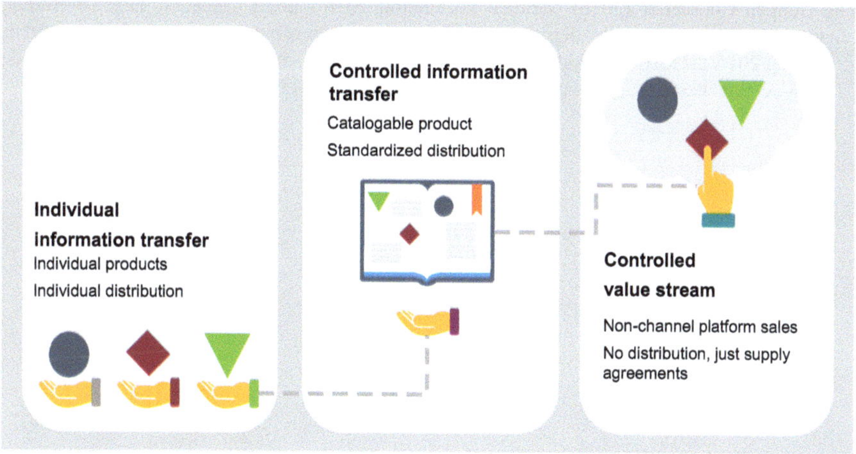


**Fig. 7.2** Transformation of business models

What is most likely to give us sleepless nights tomorrow and how can we take preventive action to counter this ahead of time?

Combine all the answers to these questions and there you have your transformed business model.

> **Focus: Transformed Distribution Channels**
> In addition to the two preestablished business models, the transformation of the business models can be effectively illustrated using the example of distribution channels (see Fig. 7.2). The "individual information transfer" category is helpful when it comes to investment goods in need of explanation. Buyers receive information for their project which is specially tailored to them. With the "controlled information transfer," catalogable and comparable purchase factors which customer themselves can learn are made available. The "controlled value stream" organizes, just like a flat rate for the Internet usage, where the end consumer—regardless of where the network connection originates—is provided the necessary bandwidth. The network operators deliver this to the customer contractual partner as needed.

## References

Deutsche Telekom/T-Systems (2015) Cyber security report 2015. http://www.ifd- allensbach.de/uploads/tx_studies/Cyber_Security_Report_2015.pdf. Accessed 17 Nov 2016

Egde.org (2016) https://www.edge.org/annual-question/what-do-you-consider-the-most-interesting-recent-scientific-news-what-makes-it. Accessed 17 Nov 2016

The German Chancellor (2016) National IT Summit 2016 – the Chancellor: Digitale Bildung voranbringen (promoting digital education). https://www.bundeskanzlerin.de/Content/DE/Artikel/2016/11/2016-11-15-it-gipfel-saarbruecken.html; https://www.bundesregierung.de/breg-de/aktuelles/kanzlerin-digitale-bildung-voranbringen-247920. Accessed 31 Jan 2017

# Digital Society

# 8

*Change has no constituency. People like the status quo. They like the way it was. When you start changing things, the good old days look better and better. You have got to be prepared for massive resistance.*

John Francis "Jack" Welch, 1981–2001 CEO of General Electric (GE).

The role of the manager in Industry 4.0 +++ Joined-up thinking +++ How to counter resistance with hope for the future +++ How organigrams and role descriptions have become counterproductive +++ Why people learn and become more intelligent +++

Managers are responsible for the key figures in their division. They ensure the availability and appraisal of these. And they base their decisions on these. They compile data in reports, create dynamic screens that provide data as well as dashboards, that access multilayered data files in real time. They are the master of this data, making decisions about programs and providing operational impetus to the departments. Just like a pilot they know about the consequences of their actions. A pilot that commands a Boeing-Twin with 550 onboard passengers, knows every cockpit control, knows about the interaction of the technical processes—but does not count technology maintenance among his duties. Here he relies on the experts, focusing solely on his piloting duties. These involve detecting turbulence and avoiding it as well as assessing risks. Similar to modern management. Unexpected situations can occur here too. Each successful day remains conditional on the use of the right instruments—but these are changing at an unparalleled pace. Reporting becomes digital communication. Previous standards no longer apply. From time to time this causes irritation.



A. Weber, *Digitalization for Value Creation*, Future of Business and Finance,
https://doi.org/10.1007/978-3-030-36229-4_8

Managers are masters at devising strategies, setting annual objectives, boosting performance figures, designing personnel development programs, establishing corporate identity, and realizing CMR campaigns. Intensive study and many years of experience have turned them into experts in these areas. But back then, when they started out, the situation was completely different. This was the time of superior knowledge and working tirelessly on your career. Those who had information, had power—that was the common perception up until the start of the twenty-first century and sometimes still today. Unfortunately, this divide-and-conquer mentality has not yet caught on everywhere—well-rehearsed knowledge is too strong. We know from brain research that a person requires roughly 10,000 h of training to become an expert in any respective profession. At one time this resulted in manager brains forming extremely robust neuronal networks. That means our learned skills can last us a lifetime. This only becomes difficult when circumstances change. Let us try an—admittedly exaggerated—thought experiment: Let us imagine for a second that this experienced manager goes into the office one morning, ready to put the usual tools of her trade to use: She holds team discussions, asks for minutes, a report and even a schedule for the day—and suddenly it occurs to her that none of her usual measures apply. Her staff refuse to the meeting and minutes, the writing of memos or notes and compliance with the bottom-up communication hierarchy. There is no date confirmation from the supplier, no phone conference with that colleague from the subsidiary, and no list of customer complaints. The manager asks for the annual objectives, but these cannot be found either because the files are no longer available. Instead staff communicate via Intranet, feed machines with data, the meeting takes place online, and the phone dictates speech into e-mails. Customer complaints no longer appear on paper, but in the form of a bar chart on the dashboard, and the corporate strategy—once a confidential document is posted across all channels for the information of all those along the value chain. All these things have now become irrelevant. Alarm bells start to go off in the manager's brain. Her brain starts firing out adrenalin. Her first instinct is to play dead or flee. To play dead would be to ignore the situation and hope that the risk might dissolve like fog. To flee would be to drop everything and look for another job. Thankfully these instincts dissipate fairly quickly. Soon reason sets in and the following thoughts start to take hold: To play dead would be suicide because no company can survive without undergoing digital transformation. Fleeing is not an option since, first of all, digitalization is universal and, second of all, it affects every little niche of life, no matter how small. With this comes the reflection period in which the German economy currently finds itself. It is currently in the process of channeling fear into action. It has recognized the challenge and is rising to it with a willingness to change. What seems to be lacking, in my opinion, is the desire to get started and, with it, the willingness to make mistakes, gain insight and make corrections. This would allow managers and staff to change their neural patterns.

While digitalization certainly is not going to happen overnight—it is happening quicker than any previous development. And that is why managers are coping not unlike the one in our example. It is only human. Why are people so skeptical of change? Why do they cling to well-worn habits, full in the knowledge that these habits are obsolete? Why does change generate stress? Well, it is brain related. If somebody spends many years training certain tasks and behaviors, then the corresponding nerve cells in the brain link up to a network. Robust synapses form and, with them, an increased confidence in one's own abilities. Change calls all that into question. It raises uncertainties because there are not yet any linked up, protein-enveloped nerve fibers. And because suddenly everything you know seems irrelevant and the new patterns do not exist. The result is hesitation and sometimes even fear. When I look at the impact of digitalization in companies, then I can understand both the hesitation and fear. The changes facing managers are immense and, unfortunately, they cannot be realized using preexisting models.

I urge you: make a start. Do not wait for polished concepts, avoid long-term objectives, do not get caught up in the details. Just do it! Fleeing or playing dead is age-old instincts that remain without effect in the digital age.

So it is only human to react defensively to change, in our case: first asking ourselves how change will feel when the focus in the workplace switches to machines, when a company can no longer regard itself as a brand island, where managers no longer adorn themselves with power and symbols, instead casually exercising management functions on a 24/7 basis. These changes are far reaching and I would even go as far as to say they are nullifying our former understanding of what management is. This is generating uncertainty at the top-most executive levels. Understandable, given that, as mentioned. The brain cannot change its synapses formation from one second to the next. It will take another 10,000 h of training for managers to add these changed standards to their repertoire—we know that from a number of studies on how to achieve sustainable success. This requires perseverance, discipline and, above all, decisive action to start this training. Only those who approach their team on eye level and say: "Let's arrange brainstorming meetings with our entire network. Everyone is mapping out the future from their desk, sharing their ideas on blogs in anticipation of comments from their peers. Let's extend the discussion to colleagues, partner firms, customers. Let's get rid of all the secrecy, it's *old-fashioned.*"

When I can for this kind of transparency in my consultancy seminars, the faces of the managers turn ashen. Fear is written on their faces. Fear of a loss of power, a fear of slipping from the top executive echelons down to staff level. But I think it is better that way. Fear can only be overcome once it has taken a sharp focus in the mind. I advise you to place your fear on the table—just for a short time. Reflect on it for one, maybe 2 h, let it develop. Imagine which unspeakable scenes you would be faced with if you were to post your trade secrets for all the world to see. Feel the pressure around your heart. Then fully exhale. Turn your shoulder sideways, away from the fear on the desk and imagine the following scenario: Google, one of the most powerful companies in the world, is investing in the field of artificial intelligence because Google sees an enormous growth market there. A number of different research groups are currently working there under one umbrella, the Brain Team. The team lands an extraordinary coup. Out of 10,000 images, a machine identified those people who were likely to lose their sight as a result of diabetes. With a match rate of almost 98%, the machine succeeded in detecting the signs of this unspeakable disease long before an ophthalmologist would have been capable of doing so. While the researchers feel that this work is still in its early stages, they gather up all their findings—and publish them on the net as an open-source project. The Brain Team pools this research "(. . .) in a kind of software library called Tensorflow, so as to stop every corporate division from muddling away by themselves and ending up with the same results in three different places," according to the *FAZ* (Jansen 2016). Google CEO Sundar Pichai sums it up as follows: "We have seen what Tensorflow can do and we believe that it can have an ever-bigger impact outside of Google." This is a way of sharing that can serve as an example for companies that want to survive in the digital era.

Visibility is no longer down to shouts of brand quality, all that matters is a benefit to the end customer.

It is no secret that the best ideas emerge when people come together and think in an open, informal atmosphere. Ideas must be voiced and combined with other ideas. This might open up opportunities for the discovery of new niches, or even the resolution of thus far unsolved problems, purely because some people put their heads together and merged their thought processes after forming a collective for a brief period. This spirit will be the architect of future entrepreneurship when guidelines and reporting pale in significance. Remember that the biggest corporate success stories began the same way. Playing with ideas, unwavering enthusiasm, an unconditional drive to persevere with the future and, above all, not to submit to the doubters. When Steve Jobs launched his first Macintosh in the mid-80s, the computer was cast in one piece. There was no modular kit system. Jobs wanted to combine design and technology. This idea was met with skepticism by the competition. If he were to have caved in, if he were to conform to the status quo, then Apple would not exist today. But he may equally have thought it was better to dominate a niche than to disappear on a huge market. Whatever the case. The rest is history.

We should not carry our imaginary fears into day-to-day business. In business it is important to focus attentions on positive developments in order to activate dopaminergic resources, thereby promoting a good feeling for what we are doing. These psychological thrillers should be consigned to literature.

## 8.1 No Science Fiction for Managers

There seems to be a culture in science and literary circles of trying to outdo one another with doomsday predictions. The science fiction scenarios that emerge never fail to astound me. I myself have read Dave Eggers' bestseller *The Circle* (Eggers 2014). His literary heroine Mae Holland loses herself between the real and the algorithm-driven world, her consciousness dissolves into a mix of humanity and data. What appears in the beginning as democracy in its purest form in the fictional digital company known as "The Circle" ultimately reveals itself as the evil agenda of the three megalomaniac founders. They want data, and they want to manipulate the world with it. Social participation degenerates to dictation, chances for all turn out to be character pitfalls. The fact that Mae had absolutely no qualms over whether or not total transparency violated human dignity really struck me. Mae was prepared to disclose even the most intimate secrets about her own parents and even to ignore her ex-boyfriend's most desperate pleas for privacy. Ultimately, she lost what people generally refer to as empathy, i.e., consideration for the feelings of others. In essence this is a denial of the right to privacy in thoughts and privacy in actions. The stokes fear, no question about that. Who wants their every waking thought to be broken down into data? Who wants their secret feelings to be released for universal use?

I believe that such scenarios can act as a helpful stimulus to the imagination. What were once Grimm's Fairy Tales have now been replaced by science fiction novels. They teach morals. As does the urgent letter (futureoflife.org 2017) posted by some prominent brilliant minds in July 2015. There is a fear that artificial intelligence could become autonomous, particularly in the weapons industry. Critical, forward-thinking voices with clout in the international community do well to highlight the potential dangers. The fact that physicist Stephen Hawking, philosopher Daniel C. Dennett, and other renowned scientists are raising their voices attests to their farsightedness. We need personalities to monitor the situation and hold up a mirror to the risks of accelerating digitalization.

But I trust that we as a society will negotiate terms for the use of technology and come to a solution together. In every phase of economic upheaval, in every industrial revolution, it has taken time to reach this point. This remains true today. So, this cannot be used as a plea for opposition to development. It is more a question of drafting the terms on which it occurs. It is furthermore a question of building the future of liberal values and applying the motto coined by Immanuel Kant to the digital era: "An individual's freedom ends where the other's freedom begins."

And so, entrepreneurs ask themselves: Where does this journey lead? What role do we want to play in a networked market and, above all, how will digitalization impact our historic corporate values? This takes us back to the field of management or, better still, project work. In the German industry this is something which is generally reserved to engineers.

## 8.2 Attitudes of Engineers

Before digitalization became a relevant factor, German engineers enjoyed recognition worldwide for their precise, robust, and enduring work. You could say that engineering was a national strength. Engineers set the standard on the international market, both in terms of an innovative drive as well as competitiveness, especially in the fields of automotive construction, mechanical engineering, the electrical industry, and telecommunications. With their research and innovation work, they boosted the economy as well as their reputation.

But today German engineers are showing hesitation. Perhaps their learned precision is impeding them. I do detect an awareness of the digital challenge. Likewise, I trust that they will find tools to shape the future. We are well positioned in this respect. But I have also noticed that this new direction is still causing them some difficulty. They are slipping in international perceptions because of their overly cautious approach. They are not keeping pace with the annual need for expansion on the markets. They risk leaving high-tech development to their American and soon their Asian colleagues who, driven by the current Zeitgeist, are pushing innovation forward innovation in refreshing ways. Here, scientific results are being used as a basis for gradual further development. They have come to the realization that technological inventiveness is based on small but surprising steps.

We need to stop trying to revolutionize the world of data because that ship has already sailed. We have now reached a point where we should be asking ourselves: Where do we begin, given the sheer abundance of technologies? How can we extract from the data the information which is relevant to us? Where are there niches that we can fill? Where are there hidden ideas that we can use? What innovations can we derive from these? Creativity works on a more piecemeal, more detailed basis, it is no longer about taking big leaps.

Now if we imagine that every company in the world is asking themselves the same questions, it is all the more odd that the German industry is opting to hesitate, rather than take the plunge. Why are no engineer teams coming together, putting their own analyses to the side for a while and putting their heads together with the Steve Jobs promise of making a dent in the universe? The stars are in alignment. But where is the resolution to give industry this drive? The expertise is there, that is according to the Association of German Engineers, which states that: "In no other country in Europe are there as many engineers of the older generation active on the labor market as there are here in Germany. At 21 %, more than one in five working engineers come from the 55+ age category." It goes on to state that: "In fact, at the lower end of the age spectrum, no other country has a lower share of younger engineers than Germany" (Verein Deutscher Ingenieure e.V. 2012).

But I want to be clear: performance has nothing to do with age. It is the mindset which counts. Modernity starts in the mind. Managers would be well advised to hold creative meetings and abandon their target-orientated strategies in favor of results. Then results would count for more than the final outcome. This type of management—results oriented instead of target oriented—fits in better with the digital rhythm because it moves in brief cycles. A target is long term and often rigid. A result, on the other hand, is an interim step and changes may be made to the next step, where appropriate. For employee management that means allowing individuals to act independently.

**Focus: Transparency**

Employees who have great potential when it comes to analytical skills often have difficulty with transparency. They do not see the point in sharing information ahead of time. Industry engineers, in particular, regard Metcalfe's law more like a vision than the truth: "the value of a

(continued)

telecommunications network is proportional to the square of the number of connected users of the system." This law, which involves transparency and user-oriented communication, applies to five levels of a digital business model (see. Fig. 8.1).

The availability of data and information is the energy that drives revolutionary transformation within the industry. Consumers leave an enormous data trail behind them. A key activity for companies in the future will be to read and comprehend these, then to draw conclusions from them. This willingness to voluntarily disclose information comes down to the personal benefit to the respective consumer. If consumers can see a benefit, they will disclose data, otherwise they will not. The connective grid is the world wide web.

## 8.3 Role Play Versus Job Descriptions

As soon as people start to shape business processes in line with their temperament, their knowledge, and their talents, neural networks will become value chain stages. These are, after all, the characteristics and talents of employees that motivate business performance. It is a manager's job to link employee strengths beyond departments. In fact: a manager who encourages staff to use their own strengths will further boost adaptability within the company. Unfortunately, obsolete organigrams with rigid hierarchies often stand in the way of this. Furthermore, job descriptions place restrictions on staff actions. I find both—pyramidal organigrams and job descriptions—to be irrelevant in a digital business world given their debilitating effect. We can learn from digital companies like Google and Facebook.

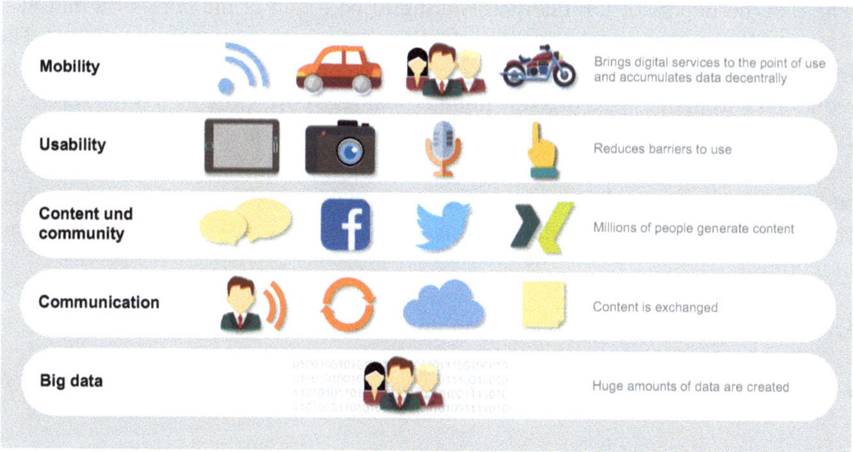


**Fig. 8.1** Availability of data and information

There, ideas are not exchanged along any horizontal line, quite the opposite in fact: Creativity is encouraged and emerges from managers and staff in equal measure in teams. Facebook has completely done away from office walls, there are only a few tables in the room, a sofa for relaxation, and free IT accessories in a dispensing machine. Consent forms are not used, these waste time and energy. This is not the case in the German industry. Here, old methods die hard in HR departments, especially the job description. For me, job descriptions are creativity killers. Their pages list employee tasks. Once set, these job descriptions apply throughout the working life of the employee. These do not change with the growing strengths of the employee and do not adapt to change. And at some point, this written language and the reality of business start to diverge.

Imagine an employee in marketing who writes the annual business report with ease. He knows the tools that make a text good. As a line manager, you are always surprised at how easily he puts even the most complicated contexts to paper. But: he cannot market this text or issue a business report on the subject in the trade and business press—despite this being part of his job description. As a strengths-oriented manager, you praise your copyrighter for his written work and assign the marketing tasks to a creative employee with communicative skill. Regardless of the job description, you look for an effective duo for this task, one with strengths in copywriting and the other in PR.

It is no longer a question of filling staff deficits with training. There is no time for that and that would contradict modern personnel development approaches in any case. Training weaknesses is laborious and leads straight to apathy for change. It is better to focus on an employee's strengths. And if your team should be lacking in any strength, you can have a look around online.

Sourcing models are playing an increasingly significant role in the world of digital business. They range from single to global sourcing and allow managers greater room for maneuver. Where there is an absence of certain skills in-house, the manager can acquire these on a selective basis. The ideal solution is hiding somewhere in the depths of the Internet, waiting to be found at the click of a button—almost. Maybe there are plans to add illustrations to the business report. The freelance illustrator database can be accessed in a few seconds and a work sample requested within the space of a few minutes—at zero cost. Only then is the service is commissioned. If we look at the efficiency factor here, it quickly becomes clear that the uncomplicated, project-specific use of expertise aided by digital communication adds new tools to production structures and enables staff to avoid wasting their energy on tasks that do not suit them. Imagine you were to ask your team at the start of a project:

- Which tasks do each of you want to do for the duration of the project?
- Which tasks can be handled ourselves?
- Which tasks should be outsourced in order to use our team strengths logically?

Even the outsourcing of tasks requires courage to allow transparency. Many entrepreneurs worry that their willingness to involve external parties and provide them with information could be misused in digital channels. We will have to live with this risk.

## 8.4 Growth of Intelligence

The future is less predictable today than it was a few years ago. Private and professional spheres are merging to form an everyday reality. People are tapping into more than one source to generate knowledge, they are using a number of channels to inform their opinions. They discuss on a universal basis. They are distressed when an earthquake happens in Haiti, mourn the victims—while at the same time a homeless person on a park bench down the road is overlooked, despite the fact they are freezing to death. In any case, it should be noted that individuals' perspectives are broadening. To stop yourself from getting lost in all this, it will be important to create breathing space away from the weight of information. Occasionally your brain needs a rest from data, it needs quiet. Otherwise you would function relentlessly in the gamma wave range, at a high hertz frequency, discovered by scientists only with the acceleration of digitalization. In this range you consume information incessantly, working in a highly concentrated mode. Over an extended period, this would damage your brain—it might even shrink under this sustained stress. Personal stress is a factor that should not be underestimated in the course of digital transformation.

Managers do not switch their cellphones off after a 10-h working day, they want to remain accessible, even at home. If anything, I see a tendency to fill the available time with more and more tasks, thereby sustaining the high frequency of the brain waves. Do not do it! This leads straight to exhaustion—and stunts your creativity. This, by the way, only emerges when you switch your brain to alpha mode, when you let information wash over you from time to time. I have gotten myself into a habit of blocking off a time window of 3 h twice a week. For my private life, for the unexpected, and for recuperation. I fight for these fixed windows of time in my schedule if need be. Initially I felt that this was idle time, but now I see the benefit. The world can cope without me for a few hours and the company too.

One finding related to the consequence of digitalization is that people regard themselves as irreplaceable and that responsibility is shared with as much reluctance as information. It is essential that your team does not feel helpless when you disappear from the computer screen. Under no circumstances need communications among one another stop! That is why I regularly hold team meetings in my company to discuss the most important communication tools for flexible innovation management. These include:

1. Chats

   These are idea for quick, informal dialog beyond hierarchical boundaries. Polite formalities can be ignored here. These are quick briefings, a digital shout, almost in passing.

2. Blogs
   These are a tool for boosting transparency. Talk about what you are doing. Present your results in articles—keep them short and sweet—while at the same time keeping up to date with other team members. These are interesting snapshots which can be merged together at the end of the day to form a performance overview.
3. Internet Platforms
   Blogs can be merged on a web platform that pools all relevant content for the use of groups with defined access rights. Different levels of confidentiality represent access rights to various content. The embodiment of networked knowledge.
4. Data Analysis
   What is generally referred to as Big Data can be decrypted with various different programs: These programs detect, probe, and link various data patterns. Data sources consist of protocols from servers, online clickstreams, social network activity or are decrypted by sensors in cell phones. Remember?

Data is the energy of the future. These communication instruments require fine-tuning too before they can reach a standard level. What is important is that you start. Learning by doing is the motto.

The human brain has a high degree of plasticity. It can adapt to new developments and add new patterns to older ones. Amazement, research, engaging with the new, weighing up advantages and disadvantages, thinking ahead, and optimism when considering obstacles all promote human performance. While an individual's intelligence quotient may be determined by genes initially, it can also be boosted by environmental factors and challenges. American political scientist James R. Flynn discovered this when he conducted his study on children in fourteen countries, the outcome of which was published in 1987 (Flynn 1987). However—and this is still highly relevant today—he pointed out that intelligence increases by an average of three percentage points from one generation to the next. Intelligence tests should be readjusted in line with this cycle. This so-called Flynn effect attracted the attention of other scientists and many found that environment, education, health, and even the mass media had an influence on the increase in the general national intelligence curve. Flynn responded to this in his book *Are We Getting Smarter?* (Flynn 2012). Here he came to the conclusion that IQs are continuing to increase, albeit more slowly. Visual thinking skills and the capacity for abstraction, in particular, have increased. So, we can only hope that the next generation will have further developed skills which are of greater relevance to the digital world.

## References

Eggers D (2014) The circle. Kiepenheuer & Witsch, Cologne
Flynn JR (1987) Massive IQ gains in 14 nations. What IQ tests really measure. Psychol Bull 101 (2):171–191. http://www.iapsych.com/iqmr/fe/LinkedDocuments/flynn1987.pdf. Accessed 7 Feb 2017

Flynn JR (2012) Are we getting smarter? Rising IQ in the twenty-first century. Cambridge University Press, Cambridge

Futureoflife.org (2017). https://futureoflife.org/open-letter-autonomous-weapons/#signatories. Accessed 7 Feb 2017

Jansen J (2016) Googles Maschine lernt ihre eigene Sprache. http://www.faz.net/aktuell/wirtschaft/netzwirtschaft/kuenstliche-intelligenz-googles-maschine-lernt-ihre-eigene-sprache-14554153.html

Verein Deutscher Ingenieure e.V. (2012) 2012: In Ingenieure auf einen Blick. https://www.vdi.de/fileadmin/vdi_de/redakteur_dateien/bag_dateien/Beruf_und_Arbeitsmarkt/2012_-_Ingenieure_auf_einen_Blick.pdf. Accessed 1 Dec 2016

# 9 My Motto for Success? Adopt a Proactive Approach

*Well done" is much better than "well said.*
Benjamin Franklin (1706–1790), American statesman.

What might work today may harm you tomorrow +++ Opportunities and risks of German precision +++ How companies evolve digitalization +++ Generational approaches to digitalization +++ Milestones are better than targets +++

Digital transformation changes all business processes, it requires the breakup of all organizational structures and calls for a whole new set of expertise. Its scope is more extensive than you and I ever assumed. I would go as far as to say we lack the imagination to predict the developments of the next 20 years. However, that should not stop you from starting immediately. Sitting it out is not an option, not in times like these. Entrepreneurs and consultants are well aware of this, but still, it seems to me they are afraid to take the plunge. They conjure up a hundred different reasons to bide their time: "We've been at the forefront of the sector for as long as I can remember. Why would that change overnight?" or "We'll wait and see how others respond." or "We're still working on the right tools for the change" or "First we need to define our annual objectives." Stop! None of these resolutions lead anywhere. Quite the opposite in fact. You are squandering your chance to secure survival on the market. You simply do not have the time to wait.



A. Weber, *Digitalization for Value Creation*, Future of Business and Finance,
https://doi.org/10.1007/978-3-030-36229-4_9

## 9.1 Decision Chains Instead of Long-Term Strategy

This realization makes working out long-term strategies redundant. At first this may sound counterintuitive. After all, the fundamental rule was always that only strategy could define the direction of your firm, and that strategy is a management tool of commitment, credibility, and measurability of success.

That was how the business worked in the 1990s. Managers had to carefully measure every word, and as soon as a strategy had been agreed in a company, it held true for a number of years. It was a guarantee, a footing, and a type of promise for the future. Today it is of limited significance, sometimes it can become obsolete overnight and collapse. What might work today may actually harm you tomorrow. Sometimes this realization can make people feel helpless. I hope you are approaching this helplessness carefully. Take note of it. But tell yourself in the same breath that not every problem needs an immediate solution, and that even small, very small decisions can bring you forward. You cannot counter the current change process with watertight concepts. There are no long-lasting strategies to guide you on your path. Nor are there any guidelines for digital success, only a willingness to abandon well-trodden paths and enter new territory will take you forward. And in my view, that is exactly what is hampering the digital transformation.

## 9.2 German Precision: A Digital Stumbling Block?

From family-run companies right through corporations, managers, in particular, have been training in the art of precision for decades. Once they had developed new products or a different company strategy, that became a long-term project. An so began the drafting of cost-risk analyses, strength and weakness tables, error sources, innovation tests, five-year costings, CRM programs, etc. Everything was checked exhaustively and down to the last detail. That remains their strength, one that has now been so well developed that it remains unlikely any other country will ever achieve such perfection. It is precisely this precision that has been the source of our entrepreneurial potential thus far. Precision is a tradition in Germany, one that has been passed on from generation to generation—above all in family-run companies. I am all for continuing to preserve this strength, but: precision must not remain our unique selling point. It is a question of adding other facets to our strengths profile to ensure the survival of German companies into the modern digital era. These facets include:

1. Letting go of old certainties
2. Scrutinizing your core corporate competency
3. And taking joy in innovation and change

This simple three-step approach can help facilitate a successful digital transformation process. Your knowledge of digital technology is less important here. This can be dealt with by IT experts and, ideally, an administrative department within the company which acts as a cross-departmental mediator. I have already explained the part you play in. As a manager, your resolution to take risks and enter new territory is key.

## 9.3 Entering New Territory

Nokia started out as a paper manufacturer before then switching to the production of rubber boots and later tires. The company would still be working with rubber if the manager had not decided to get into the cell phone industry in 1981. That was a step up to a new level of quality—and the company has remained there to this day. After producing its first cell phone in 1987, the company went on to manufacture notebooks too and is currently working on the development of apps. Microsoft has now acquired its cell phone division—and rescued Nokia from bankruptcy. Resolution and a realignment have a history in the company, and I am tempted to say that Nokia would not survive from 1865 to today without completely transforming its fields of business and thus changing its products time and time again.

Quite the reverse is true of Mercedes. The car manufacturer has added a number of facets to its core competency. The aim was not diversification or a change in products, but an expansion of existing expertise in line with the market and thus customer needs. The company identified the desire for spontaneous mobility, sharing and cost savings—and launched Car2Go. Mercedes pioneered the free-floating concept for rental cars. Customers use the vehicle within a city and leave it wherever they want. Terms and invoicing are done via the app. An inspired idea. But now Mercedes, just like other companies, needs to think ahead, to continue brainstorming. Companies must ask themselves: *What is next?*

One thing is for sure, static providers, i.e., vehicle rental firms with fixed premises for their fleet, will ultimately be left standing. The question is whether private carsharing will develop to a point where car owners share their car. Another option would be a model whereby car users send their details to Mercedes and co. using an app and, in return, are rewarded with a cheaper purchase or rental price. The decisive factor will be future customer requirements.

Companies are going to become increasingly more preoccupied with one thing and one thing alone: generating and monetizing data. This can only happen if company leaders scrutinize and further develop their line of business, if they let go of old certainties and, above all, prove themselves willing to compromise on the consistency of their performance indicators.

In the future, data will count more than products. Given that Google was able to secure a 90% market share in the search engine segment and Facebook was able to boost its member count to 21 million people in Germany alone in 2016, we can conclude that this is purely down to a smart to approach to handling data. In other words, those who are creative and use data for their own business model can benefit, at least some of the time, from a rule of management that still applies in the age of digitalization: “The winner takes it all.”

The most successful companies in the world now appear in the form of platforms—not fixed facilities. However, according to established opinion, data channels offer loopholes for assailants, and fear of these attacks is what is making managers so cagey. My tip would be: hire security experts, delegate this worry to them, and concentrate on achieving growth through transparency. As a manager in the digital age, you cannot cover every area with your own personal expertise, you cannot be an expert in everything. In many instances you must simply retreat and delegate responsibility. This laid-back approach is one of the key attributes of a good manager.

## 9.4 The Dwindling Power of the Baby Boomers

Business models that have worked for decades or even centuries in some cases are no longer set in stone. We know the reasons for this: Digitalization is seeing more and more new competitors penetrating the market—with fresher ideas. Customers are changing their consumer behavior—and opting for companies that meet their requirements. It is no longer brand names that excite them, but innovative service making their day-to-day life easier. And this fact that their own strategy, their own brand value, and own objectives are waning insignificance is worrying managers. The only problem is that fear is a poor adviser. It shuts off the imagination. It prevents solutions. Then comes irritation. You can feel it in politics, the economy, and almost all areas of life. This fear was reflected in 2016's German Word of the Year too. The Association for the German Language opted for "postfaktisch" (post-fact).

Post-fact means perceiving feelings first—then looking at the facts later. At first this approach would appear ill-advised. We have always been taught to consider the opportunities and risks, to weigh up the arguments and only then to factor in feelings before making a decision. This order no longer applies. We can no longer assess developments as such. We lack arguments for rational decisions because we can no longer rely solely on our knowledge. Now what comes first is a vague sense that if we do not change, we might see our own business model invalidated overnight by the competition. Here I would encourage you to trust that vague feeling, take your gut instinct seriously. Indulge in that fantastical new business idea, otherwise someone else will.

This prophecy is not new, on the contrary. It is one that is fulfilled a thousand times over every day all over the world. Both large and small firms alike face bankruptcy after allowing their instinct and imagination to fall prey to a vague fear of change. This is what causes the lack of impetus to act among CEOs or to embrace new values. A top-down approach is lacking. Why do I think managers are finding it difficult to press ahead with digitalization? It could be that disintegrating structures are diametrically opposed to a Baby Boomer's idea of management. They are not looking for any new means of instigating the next open exchange with staff. Instead they are putting up thought barriers, creating an island for themselves in a global ocean of possibilities, they think anything else would mean stress in the company.

Their bad decisions could actually be endangering their own careers. They could in fact be damaging their own good reputation as a manager. These observations are well placed. But even Baby Boomer managers have no choice but to take risks. Change or be changed.

Thoughts of security are a trait of the Baby Boomer generation. They began their careers around the mid-1980s, when the world economy was still split up into clearly defined sectors and companies, customers were loyal, and growth went according to plan. Those who succeeded in boosting key figures could be sure of climbing the career ladder. Creativity could always be tapped into using a combination of tried and tested instruments. In their heyday, Baby Boomer managers could refer to a portfolio of successes over the years, ensuring them power and status as well as recognition among their staff. Innovation processes took place at a relatively slow pace at that time. Then there was the luxury of taking the time to delve into new developments and check whether they fit in with the company's activities.

Baby Boomers have an advantage on all subsequent generations: they have been involved in the technological development of digitalization from the very first step. They remember coin-operated phone boxes. They saw the first cordless phone as a kind of new-found freedom in communication. They carried the first brick-sized cell phone in their suit pocket and took advantage of every model that came after. This generation of managers expanded their skills almost intuitively by integrating the technological advantages in their working process. Always slowly. Always focused. Eventually digital scheduling replaced the calendar in the briefcase, memos were exchanged for e-mails, and paper guidelines for electronic guides. And eventually teleconferencing replaced short meetings. The intranet sped up internal communications and customer databases were transformed into a detailed, compartmentalized CRM program. And then eventually came the point where managers' affinity for entrepreneurial progress stopped. The whole affair had become too complex.

What is regarded as an outright technological blessing in the private sphere, e.g., straight-forward online booking, real-time delivery tracking right up to the exact point of arrival; or the possibility of ordering custom versions of products that were once mass produced, tailored to personal preference, is no longer quite as convenient or practical from the manager's perspective. The reason for this is the fear of company secrets, fear of cyberattacks, fear of a flow of information that can no longer be monitored. Deadlock in their own company's digitalization is the result. But with this deadlock comes a risk to the Baby Boomer's own position. If they do not act now, others will decide for them. Ideally it will be their young Internet-savvy generation Z employees that push ahead. But in the worst case, it will be the competition that appears on the edge of the value chain to destroy the company's business model. But let us stay with the next-generation managers of the second tier.

## 9.5 The New Wild Ones

Next-generation managers have a reputation as the "new wild ones." They are curious, enthusiastic, and act intuitively. Whatever the technology market has to offer, they ask: "What does it do and how can I use it to my advantage?" Sociologists attribute the following characteristics to Generation Z within a business context: teamwork if important to them and they are open to mistakes because avoiding errors hampers creativity. They do, however, have a tendency to communicate on a shallower basis and retain only superficial knowledge. It is not their attention to detail that they are known for but their joy of experimenting. Now, let us imagine: what if they were to learn from the precision and depth of experience of the older managers without losing any of their exuberance in approaching new ideas? This is a formula for success in the digital era.

**Focus: Digital Management Skills**

Digital transformation requires different personal strengths from those of the past. What counts today is a combination of knowledge and soft skills, courage, and creativity. Neither a tech-savvy nerd with limited communication skills nor a boss with authority can progress a company alone. Today digital strengths mean:

- Creating a cross-departmental and cross-hierarchical network
- Using shared data
- Speaking and writing in strong English
- Knowledge of international cultural and language formalities
- Joy in the objective discussion, poetic literary monologs have no place in the digital world
- Knowing where information is generated and using it to optimize the value chain
- Having an interest in technological developments and asking yourself: "Can this development make my place of work more transparent?"
- Embracing the sharing of information
- Syncing with the fast pace, instead of getting lost in the details. Put simply: relax for a change!
- A high degree of social responsibility for teams and upholding etiquette on social media
- Willingness to organize projects yourself
- Letting go of long-term objectives and thinking instead along the lines of milestones
- A willingness to accept challenges
- Letting go of vague, non-measurable, non-assessable fears

## 9.6 Milestones on the Journey

Digital transformation is seeing a change in management standards and instruments, specifically the definition of objectives extolled by gurus everywhere. Managers must learn to say goodbye to one of their most well-loved management instruments: targets. They no longer have a place in the digital world, target setting is a relic from the twentieth century. Back then, when corporate years were still predictable, when the competition knew their place and there was still a clear distinction between sectors, there was no question about the relevance of setting targets. Teams became more effective the more predefined targets they achieved—and managers all the more sought-after, the higher the targets they set.

I myself have never been a fan of targets because they kill vision. The sole focus is on one event and all energy, all thoughts are directed solely at this. Imagine a marathon runner who wants to run a new personal record. She notices neither the spectators, the samba dancers at the halfway point, nor the radio broadcast van. She has tunnel vision and is thinking only about one thing: crossing the line in a new personal record. She does not concern herself with others. This may work in sport, but a digital company would struggle to reach its goal like this. That is because clearly defined targets no longer exist. The route does noteven have way markers.

Business leaders who think in terms of targets overlook the fact that the path ahead is not set in stone—continuing to dictate to their staff as before, remaining focused and blocking out any changes around about them. All this does it to ensure that staff can only move within narrow boundaries. No curiosity about the next fork in the road, no sideways glances, just stubbornly pushing ahead, regardless of the drawbacks. How much easier does the following approach sound? You as a manager denounce chasing targets as pointless. You might keep a general direction in mind, but allow small deviations and leave room in your plans for any unexpected occurrences. Your staff are allowed to proceed in stages, opting for paths other than the well-worn every now and then—each step bringing its own little successes, and each small success can be a milestone in the digital transformation (Fig. 9.1).

In my opinion, working with closely interspersed milestones and praise is one of the most important management instruments for achieving flexibility within companies. Setting milestones reduces the pressure of having to undergo transformation all at once. Milestones can prevent you from having to see bad decisions all the way through to the end. Working clearly in stages is more forgiving of errors and far less stamina-sapping. That provides certainty and improves self-efficacy. Older employees resentful of digital change, in particular, will become more optimistic with every mini-success experienced. They will come to regard themselves as participants and not also rans.

According to research by behavioral psychologists, this milestone tactic also allows employees to move up the learning curve. Older employees, in particular, have worked on the basis of one pattern for their whole professional career: setting and achieving targets. This has resulted in habit. Kicking this habit just because of the onset of digitalization is only possible to a certain extent. You cannot simply force transparency, flexibility, and initiative onto staff. You must open up learning

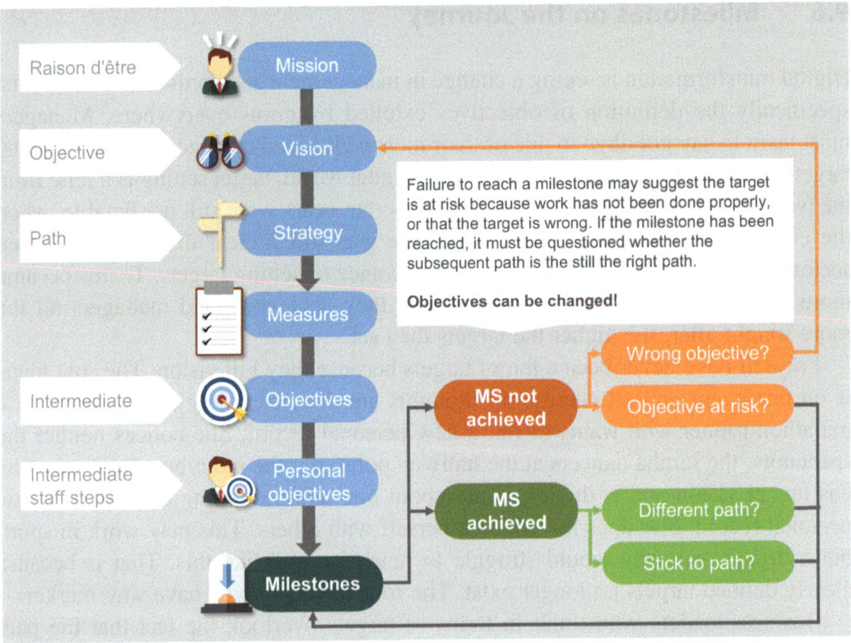


**Fig. 9.1** Working with milestones

spaces, offer them a sense of achievement. Employees will improve their skills throughout the process, in the same way that a violinist improves their ability by practicing. So, it is only a matter of time before your staff start to create change out of pure intrinsic motivation. That is why the only command you need is: go, go, go!

**Focus: Setting Milestones**
Discussions with companies illustrate the difficulty people in power have with handling change. Every beginning is hard. The model outlined helps with the initial approach to the change process.

An ongoing approach to monitoring of success is replacing the static strategy processes which form the planning process of many companies and take place at infrequent intervals. Modern and contemporary strategy processes monitor how measures unfold, they think in terms of scenarios, e.g., milestone achieved? Pick another path? Stick to path? Milestones help you to anticipate strategies and define steps that benefit the development process.

# Not Without a Team

# 10

What managers can learn from sport +++ No team equals no success +++ Make yourself dispensable—no it is not a paradox +++ How to keep improving +++ Develop a mission with your team +++ How you slip into the role of coach as manager +++ Actively encouraging innovation with the stage-gate method +++

A manager without a team would be like a football coach without players or as Formula-1 racing driver without any experts in the box. Without a team, a manager would not be able to deliver the same results. Word has gotten around that staff are the most valuable resource in the manufacturing industry and a driving force for success which should not be underestimated. As soon as managers give team spirit room to grow, they grow too. This is one of the reasons why patriarchal family-run companies are gradually starting to die out. The guiding principles of a long-successful, but now obsolete, management tradition no longer work. My advice to this generation's managers would be to waste no time in establishing an open culture, bolstered by the ideas of staff and their passion for their work.

It is not about assembling a group of yeasayers around a meeting table who will nod in agreement to whatever the boss says. That would be like paying claqueurs to shower you with appreciative words and applause. Employees would unthinkingly act in line with your wishes and do your bidding before abandoning the role of yeasayer as soon as 5 pm came. Not a shred of ambition would remain. No motivation for pending tasks. This is what you would probably call "work-to-rule." If a soccer team were to run onto the pitch with this mindset, its opponents would have an easy game. There is too great a difference between the exercise of duty and the motivation associated with a vision of victory.

An effective team must recognize and value individual strengths, it should be able to discuss with vigor and ask itself time and time again: How can I structure my role



A. Weber, *Digitalization for Value Creation*, Future of Business and Finance,
https://doi.org/10.1007/978-3-030-36229-4_10

better than anyone before me? Victory requires thinking in superlatives! It is your job as a manager to make this happen. Your knowledge of human nature and your overall view of the strengths in the team and the weaknesses of the opponents make you something of a mental coach, like a sports coach. You understand how to create cohesion in the team. Out of lone fighters, you create a team in which reliability, imagination, transparency, and a strength-oriented distribution of tasks prevail. What may sound simple is a daily challenge in business.

Especially in this time of progressive digitalization, the right tools are often hard to come by given that we are at the start of a process that is changing the world of business. Until recently strategies, objectives, the use of technology, and the distribution of tasks were solely a management affair, i.e., a matter concerning only the topmost executive level. A mission statement was put together behind closed doors—before being presented to employees as guiding principles. Annual targets to be met by staff were defined. The press was informed of any change, and staff would find out from the paper what this change meant for their job security. The result of this selective, nontransparent information policy was frustration and sometimes even subconscious refusal to engage with the company on an emotional level. As soon as the doors of the office closed behind them, the company was out of sight and out of mind, nothing more than a way to earn a living and certainly not a fulfilling joy. They sought that elsewhere, for example, participating in sport, meeting friends, or even planning a career beyond the company. Unless the managers used incentives or granted bonuses. This was known to provide individuals with a drive to perform. Only this drive was down to pure egoism, rather than an impulse to drive the company forward. Instead this performance bonus acted like the starting pistol for a race toward the goal.

Digitalization is seeing a change in corporate communications—and with it the role of the manager. A manager no longer has the role of commander or tribe chief. She is the one who, with great empathy for her staff, steps up to bring them together as a team and to get the best out of them given their available skills.

In my opinion, adopting this new understanding of the role is the first step in the digital transformation process. This includes, as a priority in my mind: identifying all the strengths exhibited by a team and embracing transparent communication. The latter is a question of trust. Firstly, thanks to communication via e-mail, intranet, digital calendars, staff chats, and social media channels, secrets will be decoded faster than the boss can encode them anyway. Secondly, there is hardly a manager out there who still has any interest in secret missions because they have long since come to the realization that, without the expertise of their team, they would be out of a job.

Nobody can run a one-man show in a complex world of business. Now managers lack the specialist expertise for increasingly complex work processes and they cannot assume the role of experts for all tasks that arise in the company. They cannot maintain proximity to every single customer and detect every problem, let alone solve them. And above all, they cannot interpret all data beyond the respective value chain stage. They lack the respective highly specialist knowledge and the time for this. They have got something much better for that: their staff. That is why managers need to involve their staff in the development of company missions. They also need to take into consideration their employees' emotions, talents, and specialist knowledge, as well as their various temperaments. They should try to form a team personality out of individual personalities. That is why I am using sport as a metaphor in this chapter. In sport, the coach acts as a mental coach who considers both the physical and mental resources of his players. Applied to industry, that means: a manager is a business coach who knows how to guide his employees from one milestone to the next by means of empathy and tactics.

## 10.1 The Digital Business Model as a Team Discipline

So, imagine a soccer coach. He takes on a team of individualists. Each player brings their own wealth of experience, each their own special skills, and sometimes even talent. One advocates a pleasant working climate. One excels in their decisiveness. Another score points for their speed. He has the gift of playing smart moves under pressure. He plays the position of left-winger, the other is an experienced central defender. As different as these player types are, still everyone must be prepared to take the team forward to ensure shared success. It is the coach's job to ensure acceptance of this and to encourage this. He must find out what distinguishes each individual in order to boost their play as much as possible. Tactics, ingenuity, and knowledge of human nature are the order of the day—and no prejudice.

As soon as the coach has assessed the mental and physical capabilities of his players and can use them to the benefit of the team, he has laid the groundwork for success. Three aspects are necessary for this:

1. Creating a good climate of mutual acceptance within the team.
2. Weighing up the weaknesses of the opponents.
3. Developing tactics that strengthen the team and target the opponents' weaknesses.

A manager must train the strengths, fitness, and speed of his team too, taking into account the temperaments of each individual at the same time. If a team member cannot adequately fulfill a certain task, then perhaps he would be better suited to another position. The rotation principle applies not just to soccer, it can also be effective in the workplace. Another member of staff would then assume this task. The game never stops though; digital processes do not offer any breaks. A well-coordinated team will deal with unexpected difficulties because it will possess a high degree of self-confidence. It has the freedom to make decisions, fill gaps, and to allow flashes of genius. Its members can rely on one another.

In essence, digital transformation will produce two types of manager: one for the wider field, where success depends on the performance of all players on the team—and one for unpredictable events when decisions need to be made quickly and efficiency prioritized. A manager needs strong staff in both areas as well as their own specialist skills, vision, and psychological knowledge. And, furthermore, they need the courage to ask themselves: where are my skills as a manager and coach replaceable? Answering this question can be painful—and yet it acts as a key to creativity and therefore adaptability. Digitalization literally asks you to question yourself.

## 10.2 The Benefit Is the Goal

There are however some other dimensions you need to add to your work as a manager. While so far, your focus has been firmly on your own value chain stage, now it is going to slide along the entire value chain. You will also have to keep the periphery in mind and live with the fear of being sidelined from the market by the competition tomorrow. If you do not manage to deal with this in an exemplary manner, this fear will be transferred to your employees. Your guiding principles may indeed state that fear is a poor adviser, but the second you fail to deliver answers to the dangers of tomorrow, your staff will start to doubt this.

I view it as a manager's duty to give his or her team optimism for the future. And by this I do not mean any neurolinguistic programming (NLP)-style slogans: "We are fit for the future." or "We can do it." Such platitudes evaporate quickly. What employees need is a model of courage and optimism. These can only be lived out in practice, not written down. That is why I view the gold-framed mission statements often found in companies to be redundant. They would be almost poetic if they were not brainstormed by several team members and tested again and again for their validity. This ongoing scrutiny functions as another tool in the midst of the digital transformation. It would be good if you were to try it out on yourself first of all. Take a step back, retreat, and ask yourself the three master questions of management, the answers to which might reveal that you are becoming dispensable in your company.

1. Master question: What is my contribution within the value chain system to facilitating the ultimate benefit?

   In an ideal society, all politicians, entrepreneurs, the church, and all citizens would ask themselves this question. It is aimed at the maxim of progressing with willfulness, self-awareness, and liberal values, not allowing mental barriers to stop you. This takes us to the concept of subsidiarity. The strength of the community emanates from individuals and becomes all the more effective where the common good is the goal. This is an optimistic approach. Managers should internalize this and give their teams the tools to adopt this attitude. It involves transparency, appreciative communication, a focus on strengths, and a willingness to view mistakes as ground-breaking. This best answer to the first master question, by the way, would be the realization that a team fulfills its duties without the manager. It would select the tools itself and make decisions within the processes. It would communicate mistakes openly and perceive the boss as somebody on the periphery that exercises a corrective function or sends signals when necessary. Viewed from this perspective, the team sets its own schedule and acts as its own manager.

2. Master question: Who could do what I do better?

   Imagine cutting your own job. I know the thought is unpleasant, and perhaps you might bristle at this internally. But still, imagine you were to fail in your career path. Who could replace you? Think hard, factor your staff, your colleagues, and your competitors from the far periphery into your calculations. What would this person do better, more cost-effectively than you? Boundless honesty is required here! Because this is how to prepare yourself for unpleasant surprises. A modern manager has an answer for every risk, even if these should never happen.
3. Master question: What do I need to be able to perform most effectively? By this I mean skills, tools, and methods. Know-how does not remain sacrosanct for life and resources can run out. As discussed in the previous chapter, I do not think much of setting major targets. Think in terms of milestones. Evaluate your success in small steps. This falls in line with the market and the accelerated pace and allows for the correction of mistakes. This is another frequent stumbling block for managers since they often check technology first before thinking about employee motivation. The order should be reversed: Get your staff on board first—then consider which technology would be most suitable for your work once the process is underway.

After this small, lonely intermezzo you can again turn your attention back to the team. Your staff too will see themselves confronted with uncomfortable questions. You must be able to react equally sensitively to any sign of failure here. That is why I am a big believer in training mental skills that prevent an individual from falling to pieces when difficulties emerge. As soon as you have formulated a plan as to how to proceed with the next steps, as soon as you are pursuing a common mission, you will identify the pitfalls on this route with honesty and openness.

## 10.3 No Mission, No Team

Digitalization changes a company's value set. Commitment to one's own brand is playing a lesser role, while transparency in communications and the linking of networks are becoming matters of top priority. Everything is being called into question and what works today might not work tomorrow. But there are some values that are more enduring. They are the soil in which new ideas grow, a constant in times of change. Employees long for that last modicum of certainty that digitalization permits, and it would be good if you, as a manager, could fulfill this desire. That is the only reason mission statements still exist. Gold-framed guiding principles, as mentioned previously, are passé, but mission statements, made from the emotions of employees, will prevail. They express in words their self-image. The answers to the questions of what your company is doing on the market and how you and your team can reach your milestones will soon replace the clunky and sometimes elaborate corporate identity in companies. Companies will forgo defining design, communications, and behavior, opting simply for a mission statement. This describes what you and your team are in a position to do and how you will reach your milestones. Like a pencil drawing, it offers a sketched outline of your path, full in the knowledge that the color can change or that parts may need to be erased or adjusted. Describing this mission is a special task incumbent on the mental coach and team coach. After all, a mission should be carried by all players on the team. And this is exactly where the difficulties start.

Generally speaking, it is assumed that an employee wants team success. But: his knowledge and experience, the belief systems on which he has acted for the past however many years, those will prevent him from following your instructions to the letter. That is a good thing. Otherwise your staff would be like robots, programmable, and predictable. But, regardless of all that laudable diversity, it is important to come up with a shared route map. So how can you succeed in adapting your team to change? Modern corporate organization theory has the following answer: seek consensus. Discuss the upcoming milestones.

After having advised you a few lines back to take some time and answer the three master questions yourself, I would now like to encourage you to move onto the next step. Pose these questions to your team in a slightly altered format. The answers form the basis for your shared mission statement which, in my experience, should apply for around a year.

1. What do you see as your role in the team and how can you generate benefit for the customer in this role?
2. A change of perspective: What role does the customer attribute to you and how can their standards and expectations be reflected in your product?
3. What would happen to the team and the customer if you were no longer there tomorrow?

**Focus: In-Team Evaluation**

A team will be all the stronger, the more honestly it evaluates its roles/tasks. The fields

- Input from manager
- Output for customer
- Mental and physical condition of team members

play a role in defining tasks/functions here (see Fig. 10.1). If roles are performed in such a way that they contribute value in line with the principle of subsidiarity, then the company has struck a balance between production and benefit.

In a nutshell: a mission statement is not a bible. It must be reviewed and adapted at least once a year. This requires commitment from your teams but not necessarily consensus. You will come across employees who do not wholeheartedly follow this mission statement. Grant your employees their resistance. Bring up the topic of doubts in the team setting. You can be sure that teams are capable of dealing with

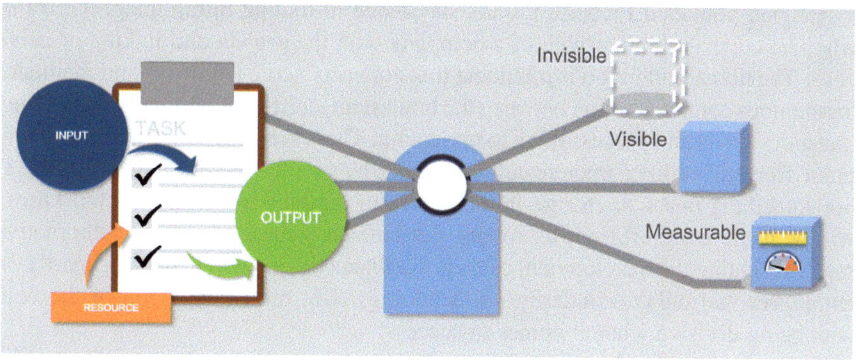


**Fig. 10.1** Impact of value contribution to a department/organization/undertaking

dissent. I have never seen a team be influenced by nonconformists or even troublemakers. A team always wants to progress on a shared path, it does not want to fight and does not want to lose. It is capable of team discipline. There may be those in the early stages that look for an "enemy" to justify their own hesitant behavior. Do not play up to this stereotype.

Say: "Okay. You have your doubts as to whether this is the right approach. I can understand that, but I can't change it. So, what I would suggest is that I withdraw from the discussion for an hour to give you a chance to table your concerns. Have your say! But it is important that you know: neither the management staff nor the executive board dictate this strategic direction, your anger would be misplaced there. I myself am the one who proposed this mission. I am sorry that I cannot fulfill each specific wish. We need to find some middle ground. If I have got it wrong here or if I should make any mistakes, we will adjust our strategy immediately. That's a promise. But first, let's make a start." Allowing an enemy stereotype to emerge only to rebut it again afterward is a common method in the discovery process before the start of a project. The important thing is that you do not present your mindset as a dogma.

## 10.4 Do Not Manage, Coach!

A company in flux is like a neural network. Synapses form, as they do in the human brain, when we train capabilities. Adaptability needs to be trained if it is to succeed. Central to this is the team, which forms an ongoing network with other teams along the value chain. Ideas and innovations are interwoven to form one data fabric. Additional dendrites form connection points. Self-learning systems emerge. The manager moderates and coaches but no longer leads. He provides stimuli, just as Steve Jobs did, for the further propagation and constant invigoration of networks. That is a corporate culture unlike any we have seen before. It is open at all ends. It is free of hierarchical structures.

Belgian politician Frédéric Laloux succeeded in finding fitting imagery for this when he compared the growth of a company with the growth and linking of nerve cells. The human brain too is a miracle that connects nerve pathways and facilitates harmonious communication between the brain stem, cortex, and limbic system. They transmit signals and process them to perfection. There is no higher power, no central brain. Remember that corporate culture is made by people—not machines, and this is not something that will change in the course of digital transformation. Workflows will be made more efficient by robots, but humans will remain in an authoritative role, facilitating the development of their intelligence. This will depend primarily on employees and only secondarily on technology. But the combination of the both with being decisive when it comes to success.

Conversely, technology can be installed, staff must be convinced. Do not be rushed by the speed of change. The important thing is not to sacrifice your creativity to external pressure.

Select tools that promote communication and reinforce understanding of each step within a process. These tools are: open, appreciative communication, the encouragement, and development of employee strengths, the creation of thinking spaces where employee thoughts can take flight and, above all, a firmly entrenched error culture.

## 10.5 The Gate Method

In order to anticipate where the business is really headed in the future, you have to be alert. Where are trends recognizable? How are the needs of the end customer changing? What could become a trend and where are countercurrents forming? Futurologists send scouts out to find answers to these questions. They keep their eyes and their ears open, sift through newspapers for vague indications, they are the trackers in the information jungle. Unfortunately, when futurologists label a trend, it is already visible and you can be sure that any competitors have already worked out the perfect plan to respond to this development. Therefore, I do not recommend waiting for institutes to make announcements. Look for signs with your team and formulate a scenario on the basis of these. This is a gate process that consists of five steps—see Fig. 10.2.

**Focus: Chain of Action Under the Stage Gate Method**

Innovations always start with ideas. Often it is the small side issues that, upon closer inspection, drive success. Under the creative stage gate method, a chain of action emerges from the ideation phase right through to monitoring. In an ideal scenario this may lead to a changed business model. The important thing is to note down ideas and develop these in the team. After this easier phase, you will be left with a clear structural line—see Fig. 10.2.

(continued)

Stage gate processes serve as a means of forming, channeling, and managing ideas. The limiting factor is the performance of companies. Depending on the level of innovation within a company, only a certain scale of ideas can be worked on, developed, and funded. This is where the risks of losing innovation come into play: at each gate there are frequently questions—direct or indirect—about whether to reject ideas.

Only two creative tools are used here.

1. Search fields

   On the search-fields level, you gather whatever you judge to be interesting or relevant. You gather ideas, facts, long-term objectives, or any flashes of genius in a shared digital notepad. This is really about open thinking, initial unstructured idea gathering, and the collation of information with minimal effort. There is space for future trends here. There will always be topics that must be developed, that need to mature—even in a time where change is picking up the pace by the day. Everyone in the team can use the notebook in different places and at different times from other team members to add their ideas to it. Not a thing is lost, no words to go yellow on paper. If you are concerned that a digital notebook might tempt crazy ideas, I can assure you: I have yet to see staff letting their imaginations go into overdrive. Their emotions always center around the relevant issues. Good ideas originate in emotions anyway. It is not until afterward that the brain examines the relevance.

   That is another reason why scheduled creative sessions tend to prove fruitless. Neither emotion nor brainwaves can be evoked on command. They make unexpected appearances in traffic jams, in the shower, at the movies—extraordinary thoughts are not predictable. The theory of relativity is said to have been the result of such a brainwave. Albert Einstein came up with this around a century ago and knocked the then generally accepted theory of physics on the head with his idea—

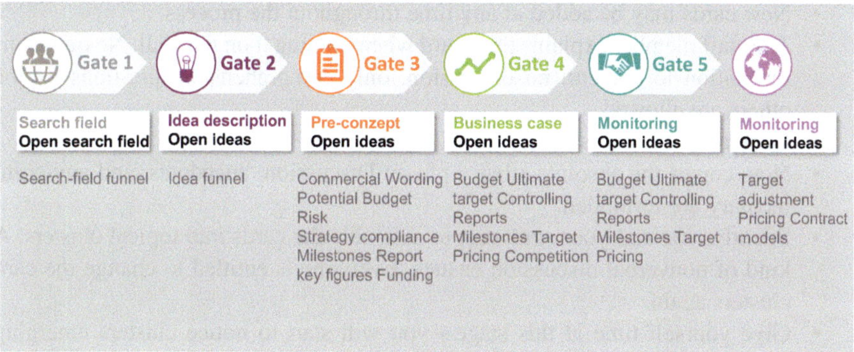


**Fig. 10.2** Chain of action under the stage gate method

that gravity occurs when space and time curve. We should be thankful that he carried his notebook with him! After all, flashes of genius disappear as quick as a shooting star. These thoughts appear in short-term memory for only a few seconds. In other words, if they are not written down straight away. In digitalization, the advantages of sharing and further developing ideas certainly stack up.

I have respect for ideas, I think they are enriching regardless of the scale in which they reappear later in the structuring process. I take great joy in interpreting these thoughts as an indication of employee strengths.

- Encourage your employees to add to the digital team notebook regularly.
- Reassure employees if they feel like a thought might be redundant or not worth writing down.
- There are no obstacles, no rules. Creativity should know no bounds. Experience has shown that even crazy suggestions can ultimately prove useful.
- Your job as team managers is to ensure an abundance of topics, to pick out themes, and to reflect on these within the meeting.

2. The KJ moderation method

Visualization, interpretation, and structuring—those are the three main characteristics of KJ moderation, which takes place on a nonverbal basis. In contrast to brainstorming, where the participants call out their ideas to the moderator, the KJ model avoids any sound. Japanese anthropologist Jiro Kawakita introduced this method in the 1960s. To this day it remains one of the most popular teamwork management tools because it takes the emphasis away from the volume and persuasiveness of extroverts. The KJ method guarantees calm and reflection and allows team spirit to grow on the basis of silent agreement. This allows it to capture feelings that would not have been able to emerge in a verbally engaged situation. Start this creative session with a master question on the meeting topic, for example: "Which tools can we use to make our work more efficient?"

- Employees write down their ideas on cards.
- An idea appears on a card.
- The employees select short and succinct terms.
- Anything goes, every idea is a good one. There are no critics and no self-doubt.
- Each employee pins their card on the wall in whatever order.
- New cards may be added at any time throughout the process.
- The staff member explains their card when pinning it on the wall. No questions in relation to content, no discussion, only comprehension questions by the others are allowed.
- Look at all the cards in silence with your team.
- Now comes the absolute silence phase: Discussion, anecdotes, and any commentary are forbidden.
- Silently, you and your staff start to assemble the cards into topical clusters. A kind of nonverbal discussion ensues. Everyone is entitled to change the card clusters again.
- Give yourself time at this stage—you will start to notice clusters emerging bit-by-bit.
- In the end, formulate cluster headings in your team.

The result on the wall is your groundwork for potential development steps. You can use the KJ moderation method, for example, to ask yourselves: "Which tools will help us en route towards the digital future?" or "How can we become the best service provider in the world?" The map for your future is already hanging on the wall in puzzle pieces. Then comes the time to sort, assess, and prioritize these. This is where you as a manager are in your element.

After this creative session, these ideas, solutions, and answers should be applied in practice. This will succeed only if you know your team. Those who give employees the feeling that they can work to their strengths, appreciate challenges, encourage, and challenge, they have understood how modern management works.

# Celebrating Success and Failure Together 11

Develop a new mistake culture +++ Why you should reward mistakes +++ Fear is not a good adviser +++ Develop unknown capabilities +++ Better to praise your staff too much rather than too little +++ Trust is good, trust and change is better +++ How to successfully set course for the future with objectivity and emotion +++

"The less mistakes a company makes, the more successful it is". That is the unwritten heading of countless mission statements. Wonderful staff philosophies about tolerance, team spirit, and fairness are everywhere but just watch: all it takes is one mistake, overconfidence, or a desire to experiment before the cracks start to form in this mission statement. Then tolerance turns into a lack of understanding, team spirit turns into a blame game; any concept of fairness disappears when mistakes are discovered. "There must be consequences," booms the voice of the boss: "Where would we be if we glossed over the mistakes of employees with a shrug of the shoulders? What we need, is accountability—and no risk." Well, the manager is not completely wrong here: success is easier to calculate than failure. Success can be measured by the factors of time and money. Mistakes/failures, on the other hand, are the stumbling blocks en route to the goal, and sometimes these can catapult the entire team right back to the start. Helplessness ensues. The manager lacks the insight that mistakes can be useful, and employees lack the composure to learn from mistakes.

Mistakes are inconvenient and, under certain circumstances, can be expensive. That remains the mindset in German companies. So please: avoid mistakes. Employees that make mistakes will be held responsible. They must justify the point and pointlessness of their actions. These discussions give the boss reason to call into doubt the expertise of the staff member and give the staff member reason to worry that a note might be added to their personnel file. Perhaps, true to his fears, he

 
A. Weber, *Digitalization for Value Creation*, Future of Business and Finance,
https://doi.org/10.1007/978-3-030-36229-4_11

will come down in the manager's estimations and be given less responsibility in the next task.

I think this way of thinking is obsolete. It is reminiscent of school discipline and methods from the last century, that have no place in a modern company. Mistakes are not flaws. They are an indication of what is possible and what needs alteration. They are a mark of engaging intellectually with a topic and thus a criterion for success. As the saying goes: Those who make no mistakes, do very little work because work involves making mistakes. Applied to digital transformation this means: those who make mistakes in times of change are demonstrating that they can approach the limits of what is possible. They are sounding out all the available options. Those, on the other hand, who overlook and impede possibilities will never have an innovative impact. They will never be disruptive. They will be sidelined!

There is just one exception in this new philosophy of approaching mistakes: as soon as it comes to the safety and protection of people and the environment, mistakes can have catastrophic effects. Therefore, I am removing occupational safety, environmental protection, and quality assurance from the following line of argumentation. Mistakes are nonnegotiable in these cases. They must be avoided, and the responsibility for this lies primarily with the employer and secondarily with individual staff members.

## 11.1 Fear Versus Composure

The digital revolution requires a changed way of thinking on all levels, both professionally and privately. Privately it is the smartphone that determines our line of vision. Hardly anybody walks through a foreign city without some sort of navigation system, hardly anybody lets their gaze wander aimlessly in public spaces. Their eyes remain trained on the information being delivered by a little smartphone. The world is shrinking in order to grow. Increasingly, communication requires digital channels. Nothing seems certain in the professional sphere, even routines are disintegrating. Change does not tolerate routine. Nobody can escape the digital revolution. I cannot imagine where they could hide.

Digitalization influences society, politics, the economy, it penetrates all systems and processes. It even influences the values of each individual. This makes a change in our way of thinking absolutely indispensable. But compulsion has never been a good basis for success, and that is why I want to start by advocating more calm. This should also involve the introduction of an experimentation phase in the transition from the analog, hybrid to the digital era, the opportunity for ingenuity to emerge, an aspiration for success and a celebration of mistakes. The joys that people share together, will not be made void by technology. This realization allows us to view mistakes in a whole new light, changing our perception of these as mishaps to potential successes. Modern companies are already talking about successful mistakes. Mishaps and failures are regarded as significant steps toward business targets. We should be pleased if we identify a mistake in complex systems. This is an indication that has understood a topic.

## 11.2 The Three Types of Mistake According to Aristotle

Hunting for mistakes has a long history. Even ancient philosophers dealt with this issue when they asked themselves the question of a fulfilling life. They approached this with wisdom, and sometimes true farsightedness. Aristotle, the celebrity among the ancient philosophers, who left people dumbfounded with his research into natural science, ethics, state, and poetry theory around 2400 years ago was said to have distinguished between misfortune, mistakes, and misdeeds. His three-mistake category has been handed down through the ages: A misfortune or accident (atuchêma in the Greek) is an unpredictable event free from malicious intent. By contrast, an error (hamartêma in the Greek) is predictable but in no way associated with evil intent, A wicked deed (adikêma in the Greek), on the other hand, is an event whose negative consequences are predictable as well as an expression of evil intentions (Wikipedia 2017).

This triad is still relevant today, some insights never lose their appeal, regardless of whether their interpretation changes. Of course, accidents do not happen as a result of evil intentions. In companies the foremost task in safety and quality management is to avoid any accident. Soft factors such as creativity and innovation are just as commonplace here as anywhere, but, like a Formula 1 pit-stop, every little handle is carefully inspected by the engineer. It is just a matter of care, practice, and drills. If I want to check a handle over, I cannot do this while it is in use. I must stick rigidly to orders. I can, in theory, check this handle over with my staff later on, readjusting it and testing it when it is out of use. But during the process itself, the emphasis must be on caution and reliability, anything else would put human lives in danger.

It is the safety manager's duty to keep the error tolerance close to zero. The five safety rules learned by every electrician in their basic training before entering the profession must, for instance, be applied here.

1. Disconnect from power
2. Secure against restart
3. Check that no voltage is present
4. Earth and short circuit
5. Cover or block off any adjacent live parts.

No freedom of interpretation. No distractions. Individual responsibility. Fault liability. These are the buzzwords emblazoned over actions like a warning. The focus is not on health in the monetary sense, just the priceless asset of health. There are two aspects here: the safety of staff and the safety of the environment, followed by the safety of products and thus the end customer.

But in all other areas beyond these protections, I advocate a change in error culture where creativity is possible and teamwork desirable. Aristotle would have said that these are the errors that are predictable but in no way associated with evil intent. In my opinion these are team errors that emerge as a result of experimenting with a calculable risk. I want to draw your attention to this modern method of management because this is where the wheat is sorted from the chaff.

## 11.3 Blind Spots in the Process

Imagine you are walking along a forest path in the dark. Your destination is on the other side of the forest, you want to reach it as soon as possible. That is why you opted not to take a detour via a country road. On the way, this clouds draw closer together in the sky. The light of the moon is obscured. You cannot see your hand in front of you nor the outlines of the trees. You do not know where the next turnoff is, where stones, shrubs, or holes impede your path. Uncertain, you remain where you are and consider two possibilities: either you wait until morning and run the risk of arriving late at your destination, or, you proceed to your destination and come to terms with the risk that you might trip along the way. Neither option seems particularly appealing to you right now. But under pressure, you might opt for the second option because you think that anything is better than standing still and then finding out that others have already reached where your destination. So, you venture ahead, feeling the ground with your feet and the close surroundings with your hands, hoping that your eyes will adjust to the darkness. Perhaps you will use a stick to push low-handing branches to the side. Maybe your hearing and sense of touch will sharpen. You accept a challenge and, all of a sudden, developed the behavioral pattern to overcome it. Internally, you are driven first of all by the fact that you do not want to let unfavorable external factors stop you from reaching your goal—and, second of all, by the less attractive thought of waiting patiently until the morning or even turning back. The situation is similar at the moment in digitalization, we do not know the specifics of the path, we feel our way alone and hope, in spite of uncertain and difficult circumstances, that we will not lose out. And yet, with every step that we take into the uncertain, we grow in confidence, because we accumulate experience for the next step, discover new aids and tools, and reveal the blind spots in the process. Knowledge only becomes an asset when we transfer it from theory to practice and train it on a daily basis. Then it grows into expertise and an interpretable experience.

In the future, management will represent exactly that attitude: giving employees a wide range of decision-making options—and giving them the choice of taking calculated risks. This is an alternative to standing still which, unfortunately, has a tendency to be overlooked. The industry seems to be waiting for the path to get less rocky. People are waiting for standards and guidelines. They want to learn from the mistakes of others. But that will not work. Digitalization is increasing the speed at which we must adapt—and with it the speed of action. Those keen to wait and avoid any mistakes in processes, product creation, and even communications will not be able to draw on the key experience later on. They will never set trends or develop solutions for problems themselves. They will remain at the bottom of the sector because they choose to run along after others, rather than determining their own path. Those who do not allow mistakes to be made during the digitalization process, thereby denying their team any trial-and-error phase, will allow their competitors to dictate the pace and direction. They are, at best, obsessed or, at worst, struggling. Incidentally, error analysis applies not just to staff. In dynamic companies, even the boss shows the courage to question their own decisions within the team and point out their bad decisions.

## 11.4 The Team in Focus

The question of where the journey leads must be answered by the team. And the team is responsible for the mistakes that occur during any journey. It is not about allocating blame, nor is it about praise or criticism, solely the shared mission of optimizing your own value chain stage and that of all your partners. That means testing the limits of what is possible, what is permissible, and what is conceivable: "What can others do better than us and how we become the best?" Such questions weed out old values such as precision and reliability at any price, making way for a new dynamic. Then nobody can use the reliability argument as a trump card to prevent change.

Corporate adaptability grinds to a halt particularly when the "gray eminences" cling to old, analog values. I would advise managers to counter such blockade attempts with a climate of openness. Let the new wild ones off the leash and see what happens. If mistakes happen, the focus should not be on assigning blame. In fact, viewing an error from a new perspective adds relevance. All those involved come together to analyze the mistake in terms of the bigger picture. Nobody is at fault or not at fault, there are no alleged intentions and, above all, no rebukes. This generally benevolent approach allows a new type of trust to grow. Trust in a static conditions no longer forms the basis. Only trust in successful transformation counts. Thus, the team regards itself as a microcosm, prepared for the question: "What value do we contribute to changing value chains?" It is no longer the tasks of individuals, but the we-feeling within a team and joint achievement that count at the end of the day.

A manager cannot dictate this spirit from above, she can however evoke this state using her exemplary role. Establishing rules of play and adhering to these even in difficult times is the best way of preventing egoism. Had the responsible bankers acted in this manner before the 2008 financial crisis, they would have announced and discussed their errors ahead of time, then this crisis would have been nipped in the bud. How should mistakes be evaluated?

1. Mistakes that a team has made together are good mistakes.
   They expand available knowledge and experience and contribute to sustainable team success, provided they are dissected and discussed and not concealed.
2. Mistakes by individuals tend to be bad.

That is because the violation of the standard has not been discussed in the team and because their determination is driven by egoism and did not result from a team consensus. And because it is difficult for the team to learn from such mistakes.

## 11.5 Weaving New Patterns

If you are satisfied, you should praise your staff. "But saying nothing is praise enough?" But "saying nothing" suggests withholding information or it can even suggest ignorance. A special achievement might dazzle for a brief time, but when nobody bothers to pay attention or listen, the good idea disappears into the everyday routine. It is not written down, interpreted, or even passed on. In time, staff will lose interest in exceptional commitment because, truthfully, even if praise is not an everyday affair and sometimes we do not have the most elegant response to it, we all like to hear words like *super, fantastic, great.* Management consultants encourage praise. Perhaps participants in motivation seminars return to their desks with good intentions of recognizing the achievements of their staff—with eye contact, handshakes, and well-meaning comments. But these good intentions tend not to continue beyond the next everyday stress.

If you really do still feel compelled to praise your staff, then you will quickly realize that they do not receive these words with nonchalance, in fact they almost apologize for their work. If, in the meeting, you cheerfully shout "Great job, Mr. Smith. The product campaign gave our sales a 5% boost. Thanks for your idea and your dedication. It is an honor to have you on my team. In fact, the whole team has earned this praise: you worked together perfectly. It is not often you see such commitment." The result? Mr. Smith's ears turn red and the team looks at the floor, embarrassed. It is high time the national modesty tradition was consigned to history. Hardly any other nation responds to praise in public as self-consciously as the Germans. Appreciative words on a one-to-one basis or in the passing are still acceptable. Then the employee can wave it aside, with a quick "do not mention it, that is my job." Although this answer retrospectively detracts from his performance, this is standard practice, particularly among representatives of the older generation. They grew up in a time where service was defined and then carried out. The framework was set out by superiors and their duty was to fulfill this framework, on the one hand, and not to exceed it, on the other hand.

Younger members of staff see things differently. They are not familiar with such codes of conduct. They are more likely to have trained their curiosity than to have ticked off any prescribed duties. The idea of picking up something from operating instructions is remote to them. They are more likely to ask: "What does this do? What is the point?", and intuitively test out the functions.

A contrast of generations. Both of these should feature in a team: the cautious staff members, the impatient, the duty-bound, and the more laid-back. This mix of personality traits creates a balance, enabling members to learn from one another. I call this "calculated creativity." This does not mean letting your imagination run away with you, but rather letting your thoughts wander and then calculating the maximum possible risk rate. A tolerant approach to mistakes emerges while the desire to try out new things remains.

## 11.6 It Is Okay to Make Mistakes

A mistake does not have to mean failure. Failure in a company should not experience as much hype as it did 15 years ago in any case when the frequency of failure was regarded as a quality marker on the start-up scene. In my opinion it is about something else: I want to rectify mistakes before failure, recognize when it makes sense to restart a project or fundamentally rethink it. I want to regard a mistake as a team endeavor and use the powers of imagination of each individual employee.

"Where did we underestimate the risk? Where did we lose sight of what was feasible? Where should be have incorporated an intermediate step? When should we have anticipated the attack from outside? Why did it not occur to us that our plant capacities had run out early?" There is a lot to be gained from identifying and acknowledging mistakes like this. Collect the answers from your staff and take courage from their expertise. According to this interpretation, you should be grateful for the new insight provided by mistakes.

This is major progress and will give you an edge on the competition in terms of your thoughts and actions.

In a team guided by a healthy error culture, doubters can pull out all the list of all the details and bring these up in discussion rounds. The creative minds among the team are encouraged to let their thoughts run wild. Any boss that engages in this dynamic exchange will regard this step as an innovative process—and give it their full support. He will direct his praise at the whole team and practically insist that staff do not detract from it by waving off or downplaying the achievement. This kind of positive attitude to mistakes will strengthen adaptability and breathe life into the company's guiding principles of tolerance and fairness. This kind of trust is the future. By contrast, the kind of trust that insists on loyalty, commitment, and immutability required by some works councils and even managers are nothing more than a dusty relic from the analog era. Looking at errors as an opportunity means that you can learn from them. An alleged setback or step in the wrong direction allows a company to start again from the same position and avoid mistakes in the future. Perhaps mistakes made will actually allow them to gain insights that more than make up for the cost of the error.

**Focus: Implementing an Error Culture**

In an unwelcome development for German engineers: desire for the sophisticated technical solutions that formed the basis for the world-renowned reputation of German product quality is, to some extent, being sacrificed in favor of speed where digitized value chains are focused on the consumer benefit.

(continued)

The realization that companies can learn from mistakes is becoming firmly rooted in corporate culture (see Fig. 11.1). The aim must be to start viewing mistakes as developmental steps on the road toward the ideal product. Intelligent error management paves the way for drawing conclusions from mistakes and developing solutions. This, in combination with a leadership behavior where mistakes are not sanctioned, creates a beneficial means of achieving new product quality.

## 11.7 The Line Between Success and Failure

It would be helpful to consider digital transformation not just as a data-collecting exercise or technological upgrade. It is, after all, a two-sided affair—and both are of equal importance: I refer to one side as objectivity. This includes machinery, technologies, programs, data, processes, and working steps along the value chain. Optimizing and connecting these is the first step towards the future. The other side involves a different kind of language. It is emotional. It describes the desire that people have to prevail in the face of the digital challenges omnipresent in everyday life. People feel overwhelmed, uncertain, they lack what we refer to as a reliable anchor. If they fear that both their private sphere and their jobs are at risk, this feeling can take its toll. Managers should always keep this in mind, because both sides, objectivity, and emotion, constitute the line between success and failure. Ideally both sides should be merged into one. This can be achieved when team concepts replace hierarchies, when people can interact with one another and when they regard themselves as proactive and not reactive.

If we expand on these ideas, then in the future each individual member of staff will become an entrepreneur within the company. Then each individual will have

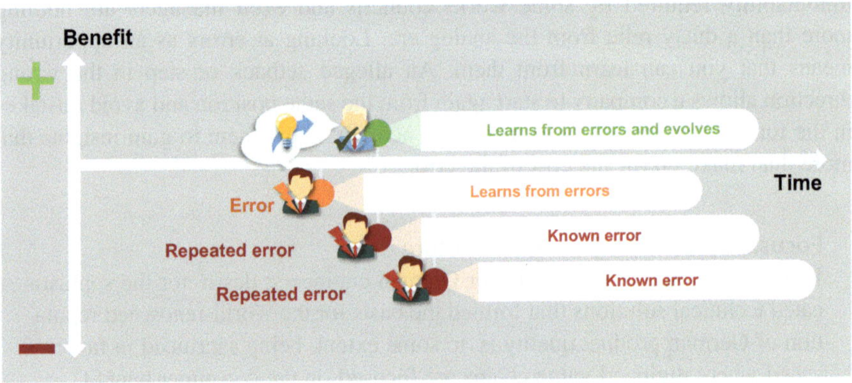


**Fig. 11.1** A positive error culture opens up opportunities

their chance to shine. Employees will not feel the need to reserve their character to appease a command unit, instead what we generally refer to as specific talents can link up. Digitalization promises a new dimension of free development and, ideally, this aspect should be emphasized in general discussion. A study by Commerzbank on the future of companies affirms this development. The study states that managers see themselves above all as motivators who attach great importance to cooperation, moderation and the reinforcement of expertise and autonomy. Control on the other hand is "out"' (Commerzbank AG 2016). And so begins the search for instruments that do not rely on a defensive attitude toward errors and sparing use of praise but an inviting gesture.

I suggest setting up an "error logbook" as an internal blog. The motto could read: "Talk about mistakes!" This type of proactive discussion can contribute to the creation of guidelines as to how such mistakes can be rectified and avoided in the future. This kind of "*best of*' book of mistakes and solutions to these will enrich your company—everyone can learn from these experiences. If that is not a reason to celebrate, I do not know what it is! But if you know me, then you know: a little celebration never hurt anyone, as long as you get back to the task at hand afterward. As you know, digitalization is happening at a fast and relentless pace—prohibiting by its own logic any hesitation or distraction on the road to the ultimate objective.

## References

Commerzbank AG (2016) Unternehmen Zukunft: Tradition trifft Transformation. https://blog.commerzbank.de/finanzwelt-verstehen/2016-mai/commerzbank-studie-transformation-trifft-tradition-110516.pdf Accessed 10 Jan 2017

https://de.wikipedia.org/wiki/Fehlerkultur. Accessed 10 Jan 2017

# 12 First, Look Inward, Then to the Customer

How customers shape your business +++ New methods of identifying what customers want +++ Stay honest, become transparent +++ Only make promises you can keep +++ Why it is important to digitize in-house before approaching customers +++ Review your partners +++ Effective crisis management approaches +++ Ethical business as a philosophy for the digital future +++

Customer questionnaires are about as sexy as discount brands at the sales counter. Both are intended to highlight a company's dedication to its customers and reinforce their loyalty. Neither of these reaches customers in the digital age. They do not want to have to tick boxes on a form to ensure good service, nor do they enjoy seeing a hundred sale stickers on a frying pan. Customers do not have the time or inclination for that. They have little interest in loyalty in any case, since that requires companies to live up to promises in the long-term. They might consider loyalty to a spouse, but certainly not to a brand or a supermarket! Why should they waste their emotions on companies? For customers, it is simply a matter of where there is a use or benefit, there is value.

A company might still reach the technophobes among its client base with traditional tools such as questionnaires, telemarketing, letters, and little freebies. But this little group is shrinking faster than the last indigenous tribes of the Amazon. So what use is the loyalty of this species on the brink of extinction if other companies have their sights set on customers all over the world?

The word loyalty is associated with a fixed or certain state. But in the digital age, nothing is fixed or certain anymore. Everything is in a state of flux, nothing is certain. Companies should view this Zeitgeist as a challenge and ask themselves what can replace this former value within the context of customer relations—my suggestion would be "benefit." This would give the concept of customer loyalty an objective


A. Weber, *Digitalization for Value Creation*, Future of Business and Finance,
https://doi.org/10.1007/978-3-030-36229-4_12

flavor. A benefit, after all, is calculable, measurable, and improvable. This knowledge could be used to add to Maslow's hierarchy of needs. If we look at the five tiers that Abraham Maslow set out in 1954 we can see that today, our basic needs are covered, safety is a given. The customer has food to eat and a roof over their heads. Now they tend to do their work on a project basis, they have no cause for concern about their next job, especially in the middle-aged Generation X category. So, the first and second tiers of the needs hierarchy are covered. Then they move up to the growth stage. Those are the third tier for social relationships and the fourth tier for social recognition and self-esteem. Before then striving for the highest tier, level 5: self-actualization, another stage should be incorporated: the benefit consideration stage: "How can I satisfy my needs as quickly as possible, on my terms and in the best environment?" is the question that the modern-day person would ask himself or herself. It sits like a transparency over the stages of the needs hierarchy. To find answers, the customer looks online. A few clicks online are all it takes to find virtual spaces, social networks, and platforms to satisfy their convenience. They can express opinions, irritation, or their requirements. They can search, buy, and communicate. They can use this mode of communication to shape their profile, thereby ensuring that their online data trails are read and noted. This would help ensure that their benefit requirement was covered. Companies that understand this will rip up their CRM instrument questionnaires and consider how they could respond digitally to the customer on this new level of the needs hierarchy.

## 12.1 I See You

Customer profiles are created digitally these days. They consist of data generated online. You can rest assured: data does not lie. It has never been easier to piece together a customer's personality profile and use this to address him or her individually. Even customers are rendered speechless when they see how accurate these profiles are. As soon as you analyze and link up the data, you are capable of predicting even the future requirements of your customers—thereby securing the future of your company.

If compiled from a variety of channels, cumulative data can tell us a lot about a customer. This is because customers express their opinions with regard to manufacturers, products, quality, etc. in various different ways. They use social networks and countless rating platforms, they comment with reference to topic, usage, and user, they provide indications of their future needs and any shortcomings perceived presently. With every like, every complaint, and every single click on your portal, the customer helps you to interpret their data pattern. Essentially it is your customer whp provides digital business ideas. This makes it all the more astounding that this corporate data treasure is hoarded in silos, collecting dust.

## 12.2 Under the Surface

Even if the customer does not always clearly express themselves, with a little imagination you can sense what they mean. If we apply Paul Watzlawick's iceberg model to digitalization, the importance of recognizing what is happening beneath the surface still applies, even in the modern business world. The iceberg model, originally a psychological model for exposing communication risks in the analog world, states that when you communicate with your counterpart, you perceive only 30% of their personality through words, gestures, and voice. The other 70%, namely desires and subconscious intentions, bubble away under the surface. They remain unseen. Not until these subconscious, unseen parts have been discovered and taken into consideration can communication be holistic. You can apply this 30–70 formula to the digital world too. In terms of communication with the customer, this means: do not restrict yourself to analyzing the sentences they use, spoken, or written. Read between the lines too.

**Focus: Customer Communication—Understanding the Customer**
A customer's personality expresses itself not in what he or she says! Discover the customer's hidden inner impulses by asking yourself:

- Where do they click and how frequently?
- Which platforms do they use to make comments?
- Which topics do they touch on, which ones do they linger on?
- At what time of day or night are they active online?
- Which emotions do you detect?
- What tone do they use to complain on which rating portal?
- Who are their so-called friends on social media?
- What is their personal time cycle? Do they rate your service before the delivery driver has even got back into his van or do they take the time to try the product out first before rating it? Are they impulsive, hesitant, reflective?
- What exactly do they criticize, what do they praise, and how can you draw conclusions from this in order to optimize your value chain stage?
- Does their complaint or praise relate to your value chain stage or another part of the wider value chain?

Customers are now communicating exponentially quicker than they used to do (Fig. 12.1). All it takes is a few seconds to verbalize a negative feeling in words—or likes, dislikes, or emojis—and communicate this irritation to an unlimited number of other customers and the competition. If a customer is dissatisfied, they will not seek a dialog with you. They do not want any consolation or compromises from you, all they want to do is get their

(continued)

frustration off their chest online. The absence of a benefit has annoyed them! And this behavior makes individual customers very powerful. In real time they can explain to an unlimited number of users what it is about your company or your product that displeases them. This will be read by other customers, competitors and, furthermore, every individual link in a corporate value chain and they may weigh in on the situation too. A message like this will leave cracks in trust on all levels. Worse still: your competitors will gain free ideas to help them review and optimize their own products and services, and to discover niches that you have not yet identified.

A few years ago, customer communications remained the exclusive knowledge of the vendor. These days are over: now, with the digitalization of everyday life, virtually every action leaves behind a digital trail consisting of an abundance of data material. When implementing customer benefit-focused digital value chains, the main task for companies is to collect, compile, and analyze this data—consisting of active and passive customer communications—and get to know customers and their interests. This information can then be used as a basis for making valid predictions with regard to the development of new products.

Just a few dissatisfied customers can cause a company serious problems and endanger its business. So, a word of advice at this point: before seeking a dialog with your customers, get to know them first. It is important to know how they are

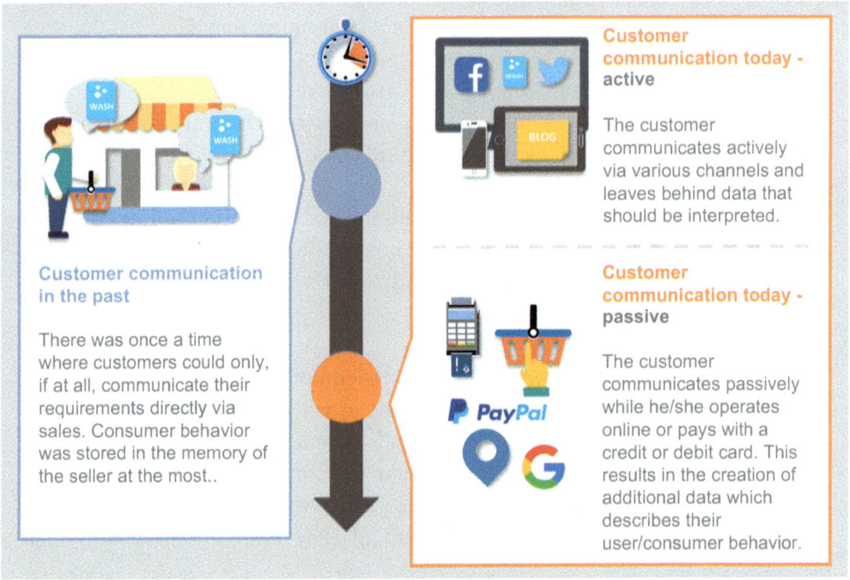


**Fig. 12.1** Customer communication through the transparency of actions

behaving today and how they will behave in the future. You need information about their everyday activities, their preferences, and their weaknesses. I am not a big fan of set-in-stone key account plans. This is too turbulent an era for those. One thing that you should map out within your company is a dynamic dashboard that outlines your customer's opinion and activity profile. Evolve with your customers. You should use a variety of different sources to find out what people are talking about and what issues bother them. You should be able to recite the media headlines as well as interpret the expressiveness of trends. You should take an interest in sociological issues and analyze those that speak to lifestyles, traditions, and new models. You should condense customers' behavior in the analog world with that of the digital world to form one behavior pattern. Why is a customer not rating your product? Why have they left your website after just a few seconds? Why are they complaining about the competition? Why are they ignoring your presence on the market? The answer is that the benefit of your offering is probably not immediately recognizable to the customer. Your task is to change that and to indicate this benefit by the most direct means possible.

## 12.3 How to Say a Lot by Saying Little

Customers are drowning in corporate messages. But digital communication should not be confused with omnipresence. Those who post online on a mass-scale, send newsletters, overuse flashing ad banners, and feature nothing other than assertions in their advertising messages have failed to understand the trend. The individual benefit is not visible to the customer—and so you remain of little interest to them. Digital communication means reflecting the customer's life reality online. If the value you are generating suits, you will gain their attention.

Then the customer checks whether your claim matches up to their experience. If the response is positive—a decision is usually made within a few seconds—they will remember your credibility. And, vice versa, if you do not communicate the value you can contribute with your goods or services, this will not happen. And so, your company disappears from view. Once upon a time, customers only needed to be won over once. Nowadays they need convincing of the beneficial value of your product or service time and time again. And you must be able to convey this benefit to them with a clear and plausible message. Cheap advertising claims no longer work in the digital era. Simply claiming an alleged added value for your customers without any proof is like announcing in your guiding principles that you cultivate a multicultural vibe in the company, despite only employing staff from the local area. Then the claim departs reality and becomes nothing more than a platitude. Advertising claims without substance have a similar impact. With that in mind, my advice to you would be to opt for a more understated customer approach for the duration of the digital transformation phase. Your strategy should involve a transparent external communication function. But before you apply this, I ask that you bear in mind the following:

1. Define your values, your customer benefits, and all the added value you contribute.
2. Add customer behavior to your dashboard by collecting facts and figures, determining needs, and drafting concepts for the satisfaction of requirements.
3. Involve your staff in this process: train yourself for transparent communication by determining:
   - What do we contribute to added value?
   - Who communicates on which channels?
   - Who assesses and monitors the customer reaction?
   - How can we form interfaces with the upstream and downstream value chain stages?
   - Are there interfaces with other parts of the value chain, and how can these be digitized?

Before you set up your external communications, each employee must understand what digital transformation means for his or her job, department, the value chain stage, and each subsequent interface. Predicting mistakes, admitting to them, and solving them creatively will remain a topic of key significance both throughout the transformation process and beyond. Opening up to the market too early can, after all, be damaging. That was the bitter experience of games magnate Nintendo when it advertised its digital game "Pokémon GO" as a new innovation. After a successful beta launch phase in selected countries, Pokémon GO went online on June 6, 2016. Simply by downloading an app, players could create virtual imaginary figures and transmit them to their own exact location in reality using Google Maps. This mixing of fiction and reality struck a chord with young people everywhere from China and New Zealand to the USA and Europe. They hunted the Pokémon of others with their smartphones. To users in their 1920s and 1930s, it probably made them nostalgic for their childhood, when they were fascinated by the Gameboy and older Pokémon games. This was supposed to be a revival. And because the enthusiasm was blowing up exponentially on social media, a few days after the launch of the game it emerged that the initial success of Pokémon GO exceeded the expectations of its inventors and the server capacity almost 50-fold! Nintendo was temporarily overwhelmed by the requests of users, released the app in just a few countries initially—and incurred the wrath of countless users thanks to poor server performance. This put a major dampener on what had been a brilliant start. This individual success damaged the business's success as a whole. Retrospective analyses concluded that the creators had underestimated the customer emotions.

Emotions can to a certain extent be explored using data but never fully. Communication is required for this. You should also talk to your staff, business partners, and customers about topics that seem mundane but bear relevance to the data world. In my own personal experience, it is not just your own conviction that counts, the feelings of others must be factored into the equation too. Keep the entire value chain in mind. Scrutinize your interfaces with suppliers and partners. Analyze the different stages of your performance right up to the end customer. But always start your communication strategy with your staff. Always ask the question:

What do we personally feel in regard to the next digital step? Where do doubts register? Where is there excitement and joy emerging? Have we forgotten any minor aspects?

**Focus: Internal Communication**

Internal communication is characterized by a high degree of transparency. It is no longer a question of passing on information that has been filtered down the hierarchical levels. The divide-and-conquer approach is a relic from days gone by. Employees are now involved in each individual process step. Specifically, this means that staff need data, information, and the competence to act. As a manager, you in return require the creativity of your staff when it comes to breaking this data down into individual working areas and utilizing it. The following tools can help you to involve employees and set up a transparent communication culture:

1. *Keeping an open mind.* Write to your staff to tell them what you have planned, what your intentions are and where you see the next milestones and what you are doing. Describe, for example, how you intend to improve your relationship with the customer and expand your sphere of influence on the market. Describe the idea behind digitalization, and what visions you have. Share your discussion with customers with them. Specify the advantages for staff. Describe a future workplace.
2. *Visualize* your digital project by illustrating these stories with graphics, images, and timelines. Employees with strong analytical skills will be more responsive to this type of argumentation than any narrative elements.
3. Set up *project blogs* where employees can post what motivates them, what they have discovered and, in doing so, pick up points. A blog also allows room for critical voices. It should be moderated and commented on. Some staff members would find this form of expressing their opinion easier than raising points in the meeting room.
4. Encourage your employees to add ideas to an *innovation strategy*. No one is as deeply rooted in the process as your employees themselves. Use their know-how and, above all: take note of any throwaway remarks. These may indicate the source of any errors or extraordinary innovation. A digital folder for any suggestions or hints may be helpful here.
5. Make *dashboards* accessible to all internally. There is just one exception: not yet approved and unreleased finance situations. Everything else should absolutely be transparent to all staff.

The more you as a manager embrace open communication, the more likely staff are to act transparently. Communication will become a common goal for which every employee bears joint responsibility. Superior knowledge will be a

(continued)

thing of the past if you contribute to a change in corporate culture with your exemplary conduct. If you keep this knowledge to yourself, it will wither away in your own personal treasure chest. Sharing it will not see its value diminished. It will have the opposite effect: duplication.

## 12.4 Obstacles Outwith Your Own Value Creation Stage

As soon as your employees come to terms with change as a model for the future, you should direct your attention to partners and suppliers. Then it is a question of saying: "Internally we are ready to take the next step digitally. Let us now consider the interfaces we form with the upstream and downstream stages of the value chain. Are these already adaptable?" You can ask yourself whether, for example, you and your upstream supplier could initiate the online dispatch of your products together. What might sound like a logical consequence of process digitalization may however lead to difficulties. The supplier can either react dismissively or openly:

(a) Either it will not yet be ready to go digital, feel slighted, and brush the idea aside, or
(b) It too may be willing to undergo change and wish to discuss the initial steps with you.

In the first case, you must consider whether this partner is still the right fit for you. In the second case, you should already possess the necessary experience to get the joint project up and running. In both cases you will have involved staff across departments in the upcoming change, so you have the power to act! Here again, if you communicate externally what you are not yet in a position to do internally, you will lose credibility and become vulnerable to attack.

Before announcing your digitalization process to partners, you must have made the preparations and run through the worst-case scenarios. You must first of all provide the necessary resources in-house and ensure the necessary expertise, otherwise your announcement will be exposed as a bluff. One of your partners might also potentially broadcast any not yet finalized plans along the rest of your value chain until even the end customer finds out about your bluster. The rapid availability of information online is both a blessing and a curse. In the era of digital communication all that matters are facts—not good intentions.

And vice versa, if your supplier should reject your suggestion of a joint digitalization project—perhaps because it is "not ready," you should not allow this to stop you from moving forward with your knowledge advantage. Your mission remains to play as effective a role in the overall chain as possible, this applies to all links in the chains. If any one individual link in the chain puts its success at risk, it must be replaced. You will bypass this link in the value chain and approach the next supplier.

You yourself will take on a disruptive role. You must keep the entire chain in mind. After all, it is only as strong as its weakest link. If you do not do that, sooner or later some else will do it for you and—depending on their position—may even call you into question. This is, incidentally, the only way to survive in volatile markets. Do not forget: all this is for a reason: creating benefits for the end customer.

## 12.5 The Dark Side of Communication

I believe that companies are well on their way to setting up practical digital communication strategies. However, various surveys have shown that many managers have their reservations. They are of the opinion that transparency can also have a damaging effect. This fear is two sided.

**1. Fear of Data Theft**
Of course, you can never rule out the risk of an employee "stealing" from you by passing the information on. Everyone is vulnerable to that. But I do not agree with shutting oneself off in premature anticipation of an attack. That would be like hiding your money in pillowcases in case of bankruptcy. An outright assurance against all life's adversities has yet to be discovered and is unlikely to materialize in the future. Yet there is a strategy for preventing data theft within companies: clarification and trust. You can clarify that data constitutes a corporate asset. You can explain that the company could incur serious damages if this were to be unintentionally leaked to the world on a viral scale. You can appeal to their honesty. What you cannot do, however, is shut your data away because this will turn your data into dead data.

**2. Fear of a Shitstorm**
A crisis can cause serious damage to a company. A message spreads through the Internet like wildfire, people share it, comment on it, and add nasty criticism to it. A company's image can be left seriously dented. Sometimes it can take years until the former image is regained. The bad news is, if this misfortune befalls you, there is no adequate defense. There are no tools for that. If you ask for an anti-crisis strategy, the responses generally are: sit it out, clarify the situation, and formulate a rebuttal. There is significant confusion around this issue, and I will often be asked: "What emergency measures should be employed when faced with this kind of crisis?" My answer? Apply your standard crisis management tactics to online PR disaster management:

1. If it happens, sit up and take note. Do not deny it, do not wait it out. Crises do not go away overnight. They pick up speed and often rage across a variety of different channels.
2. Do not response frantically. Hasty or spontaneous retaliatory action generally does little more than add fuel to the fire.
3. Set up a crisis management division. The press office alone will be overwhelmed. These situations call for more than PR work.

4. Draw up a worst-case scenario: try to imagine what the extent of the worst damage could be.
5. Tell staff, partners, and suppliers about the attacks against you. The same rules apply here: *first, look inward, then to the customer.* It is important to note that staff should not learn of any emerging crises from social media, nor from the press. Explain the situation to them honestly, before instructing them not to comment on the matter. Each employee should be obligated to maintain silence and to refrain from giving out any information. Only the crisis management team should be authorized to draw up or publish any statements or conduct meetings with the media or customers.
6. Make sure any responses to media questions are noncommittal. In other words: say that you are taking the accusations seriously and are working intensively on a solution. Do not embellish the facts, speak the truth, and do not mention any specifics. In the event of defective products, initiate the recall campaign immediately, apologize for any mistakes, and set up a credible media and PR effort. Prepare a statement, but do not respond to individual posts and do not, under any circumstances, get caught up in providing overly detailed answers.
7. Delay interviews. Journalists have no interest in averting damage to your company's image. Refer to the press release approved by executive management and promise an interview as soon as you have gathered more information on the issue. Anything that you say ad hoc in a press conference can be taken out of context. That could further fan the flames of the crisis.
8. Try to win the media over by publishing an objective press release. Avoid making any accusations yourself. Avoid any emotion, even though a crisis like this could bring tears to the eyes of any manager. Simply remain objective.

**Focus: Code of Conduct in the Event of a Crisis**

- Crisis situations are sometimes referred to as "shitstorms" in the digital world. You should have resources on hand for this. Form a crisis division and assign this responsibility for the respective crisis.
- With an external calm and internal transparency, you can prevent the worst from happening.
- Like emergency services attempting to divert heavy snowfall around a village during an avalanche, you should try to avert total damage. Your staff form the barriers, in this case, provided nobody allows even the smallest shred of information to be leaked externally. This is an exceptional situation where silence is a must.
- Keep staff up to date behind closed doors. But do not show any fear nor any sadness. Face your staff with a hopeful attitude that everything will calm down again soon—regardless of the extent of your own emotional strain.

Anyone who has ever experienced a crisis like this or struggled against a loss of image might ask themselves whether they could not prevent it from happening again by reigning in some transparency. Why disclose what you can keep secret? Why admit difficulties that are not in the public domain? I would advise against such strategies. While I can understand these thoughts, still I would not like to encourage anyone to take the road of half-hearted transparency. Even the most minor shams are uncovered in the digital era.

Just as you collect data about your customer, your customer wants to know who you are too They want to find out the idea behind your image. Particularly in times of crisis, they watch you with growing interest. They want to decide every day afresh whether you are worth their attention, time, and money. You can rest assured: the customer knows you! They know about your strengths and weaknesses—and they talk about it online. If you try to take them for fools by withholding information for strategic reasons, they will become uncomfortable. As long as you fit in with their concept of the word, they will be satisfied and accept you as an entrepreneur. As soon as that changes, they will disappear without a word. Or, even worse, i.e., if you have really annoyed them by your lack of information, and the disappointment has exceeded their subjective pain threshold, they could give you a bad rating on an online portal, insult you on blogs, even launch a campaign against you. Then they might actively search for gaps and errors in your communications.

Transparency is the only option. And this will pave the way for an extremely valuable corporate culture in the future. Quite simply, if you do not want an event to become public knowledge, ensure that it does not happen. This should become a general mindset for everyday life. My own personal motto is: "If you don't want something you are doing to come out in public: STOP DOING IT!" Ethical business, that will be the philosophy of the digital future. President of the World Ethics Commission, Hans Küng, wrote in "A Plea for Personal Responsibility" that ethical business refers in this case to proper, respectable, and legitimate economic activity (Küng 2010). This definition can be applied directly to digital transformation within companies.

## Reference

Küng H (2010) Anständig wirtschaften. Piper, Munich

# Management 4.0

# 13

What Management 4.0 means for you +++ Together, economy and politics can secure the future +++ How to deal with skeptics and grumblers +++ Adaptability is the key to the future +++ The company as a network +++ It helps to talk! +++ How to successfully counter the risk of disruption +++ The first steps on the road toward the digital agenda +++

Management 4.0 is a synonym for adaptability. Stimulating, training, and fine-tuning it is the number one task of any manager in the era of digitalization. The tool for this is communication. This, incidentally, takes place on a number of levels: by looking into the eyes of your peer, by perceiving emotions—and moreover by trusting that the spoken word can act as a steadfast anchor in this era of digital acceleration.

It is you that must cast this anchor, not management executives. They are not generally exposed to business on a day-to-day operational level. Nor any staff division, given that it is unlikely to be familiar with the team dynamic. Even an external consultant, often hired in the capacity of a motivator in difficult phases, will struggle to generate any success here. A consultant may be able to provide the impetus for action in a kick-off event. They may rouse enthusiasm for change among your staff for a moment with their words. But they cannot guide change in the long term. Their role is usually limited to the initial introductory stage. Ideally, they can perceive from the employees' facial expressions whether they are hesitant or even hostile to a transformation.

After all, communication, as any consultant knows, does not just take place on the surface. True emotions, even subconscious thoughts, emerge only on closer inspection. An experienced consultant can recognize any fears staff might have in relation to change. A nod is offset by a furrowed brow, an answer is followed by a shrug, and the corners of the mouth lift to form a formal smile. A voice is too loud or too quiet, sounds slightly off. Signs like this say more than words because these are an outward



A. Weber, *Digitalization for Value Creation*, Future of Business and Finance,
https://doi.org/10.1007/978-3-030-36229-4_13

expression of deeper thoughts. Mirror neurons do not lie. A consultant can interpret them, but steering these in a positive direction requires ongoing training and intensive discussion.

With this in mind, you should, ideally, enlist the experience of a professional in the starting phase of the transformation process. You could learn a thing or two from a mental coach with the appropriate training. Whether corporate transformation or sport, the same rules apply: If all those involved do not get stuck into a project, if they do not train right up to the limit of their comfort zone, top performances will elude them. A football team will not become European Champion if it has not grasped the fact that it must overcome its fears and sustain injury every now and then. No athlete, racing car driver or gymnast will ever reach the first division if they do not factor in failure and if they interpret injury as drama rather than an indication of a mistake, failing to analyze the reasons for this too. A company will never grow if it does not take the moods, reservations, or criticisms of its staff seriously and aim to channel these emotions down positive pathways. Make this your priority—ideally with a few professional support sessions in the initial period. Afterward you personally are responsible for team motivation, collaboration, and optimism that the transformation will be a success.

Just like a coach, set out the plan for the next game and push the boundaries of performance using mental and professional coaching. Approach staff and find out where they stand. Take the time to talk, how else are you to sound out their joys and hardships? Unfortunately, in reality, these talks are often no more than lip service. In many companies they are classed as a low priority, falling victim to the hectic pace. That is the cardinal sin of many managers. Because without face-to-face communication you will fail to identify the emotions of your staff. Your team might function professionally, but on an emotional level, it might struggle. These mistakes do not feature in a functional management 4.0 setup.

## 13.1 On the Fence

If we are to believe studies on the subject, digitalization is steering German companies toward the future at full speed. There is indeed a willingness to lay the technological foundations for change and exploit these. There is also a great desire to ensure the survival of Germany's economic muscle into the new age, guiding it on the basis of science. The one thing that is lacking however is intrinsic motivation on the part of managers and staff to train skills in adaptability. Transformation is not brought about by changes in political framework conditions, nor by scientific theories. It occurs in people themselves as soon as they feel enthusiasm building inside them from milestone to the next, thus fully embracing digitalization.

Politics has now become more of a sparring partner than an obstacle, having recognized that a more digital economy is a more successful economy. This is apparent from the disintegration of data barriers. At the 2016 IT summit in Saarbrücken, the German Chancellor was quoted as saying: "A sparing use of data cannot be the general practice for new products in this day and age." She went on to say that while there are reasonable new data regulations in place on the European level, care must be taken here in Germany to ensure that these are not interpreted so restrictively as to prohibit our big data applications. "We Europeans are known for our love of prohibiting things" (Maushagen and Severin 2016).

So far, so good. But why does Germany have a mediocre performance when it comes to digital transformation despite all its investment in hardware and software and employee training? It is the emotions of employees who have come to a standstill. Corporate digital strategies factor in investment, regulations, and guidelines, but they overlook the emotions of employees. Often what I feel is lacking is an appeal to the emotions of employees. Many seem to overlook how important enthusiasm is when it comes to reorganization. Managers have a thankless job. On the one hand, they are acting on the instructions of senior management to implement this major future project quickly and permanently. On the other hand, they have to motivate their team. They must be clear to themselves and their staff that this future project consists of countless tiny steps, that the next restructuring measure will be followed by another, and then another after that. The process is not a journey, but a timeline full of surprising events. This is what makes modern management exciting.

Unfortunately, willingness to change and the enthusiasm to do so does not materialize overnight. One meeting will not suffice for this, and targets do not apply here. The current resistance to digital change is too great. Why? Quite simply, because people fear that they personally stand to lose out when it comes to their job. The only way to counter this is to approach your team and ask for their trust, by using the first tool of management 4.0 and prioritizing communication over strategy. Offer the opportunity for discussion. Take the comments, objections, and tips of your team as seriously as you would an instruction from executive management—urgent and to be resolved as a matter of immediate importance. I know that this will not be without its problems for you—it takes up a lot of time, which is in short supply as it is. But please remember that your team is the most important resource in change.

You can probably picture the troublemaker in your team repeating his reservations over and over like a mantra while you start to lose your patience. Still, you should take the time to appease this member of staff and win him over to your way of thinking. You should take his feelings seriously and understand that any manager who enjoys a high degree of trust within their team has already established adaptability. A team that can trust, can adapt. That is because its members know that the manager is taking their feelings into account. And also, because they have learned that mistakes are celebrated and that everyone can act according to their own individual strengths. If despite face-to-face communication, and all your attempts to get to the root of these reservations, these employees still fail to get on board with the transformation process, then the time will have come to assign these individuals other tasks. But still you should not let the criticism of this employee go unnoticed. Employees who are particularly critical and often stubborn hold up a mirror to you and I am a great believer in taking note of this and asking yourself: Is there a grain of truth to this? Is there are warning in this? What do I myself need to change? Remain keen eared and responsive. You must retain the ability to question your own decisions in the wake of any drawbacks. Make clear in your stance that there is only one path for the company—and it involves digital transformation. Your priority is to establish a positive, forward-thinking mindset, not to wallow in self-pity. Perhaps this employee's happiness lies in another position, maybe even in another company.

In order for adaptability to be converted into entrepreneurial discipline, your staff need three things:

1. The knowledge that they are needed and that they are valued.
2. Encouragement of their strengths.
3. A plan for the future that takes into account both emotions as well as strategy.

## 13.2 A Plan for the Future

I have already pointed out that it is almost impossible to predict the future. This leaves us with the question of which pointers we can use to guide us. The bad news is, there are none. Key figures and core expertise are no longer reliable benchmarks. Entrepreneurs cannot simply roll up their sleeves and decide to shake up the market with advertising and image campaigns like they might have done 30 years ago. Neither of these approaches will wash with the customer these days. Your company name and all your brand campaigns will go unheard as soon as the customer sees his needs fulfilled more effectively, more conveniently, and for a more reasonable price elsewhere.

In these times of uncertainty, there is only one way to survive. You must not tire of looking for errors in your value chain stage and remedying these with new solutions. Every now and then you must take a step back from your work and ask yourself:

"How can we become even better, how can we accelerate the transformation?" I believe that this distance from your own work is necessary in order to enable ingenuity—now more critical to success than ever. "You can't connect the dots looking forward; you can only connect them looking backwards. So, you have to trust that the dots will somehow connect in your future. You have to trust in something—your gut, destiny, life, karma, whatever. This approach has never let me down, and it has made all the difference in my life." (Jobs 2011). These are the words of advice that visionary Steve Jobs sent alumni on their way with at their graduation ceremony at Stanford University. He was right. We need the freedom to think creatively, room to learn, and sometimes a little distance from the problems at hand. Only then we can see the consequence of our actions, or individual situations come together to form one meaningful whole. Likewise, adaptability cannot occur until we are prepared to stop and consider who the main characters in digitalization are: you and your team! Each individual brings their knowledge and emotions to this project, gearing their commitment toward milestones, and thereby forming part of a neural entrepreneurial network that boosts their synapses with every new skill learned, every mistake, and every milestone achieved. Monetary investment in digitalization pales in significance in light of this. The main priority is recognizing the emotional moods in your team.

## 13.3 Employee Fears

Not only will digital transformation change your company but it will also change the everyday life of your staff. So, it is only natural to encounter some resistance at first. If someone is not blessed with a great deal of curiosity or adventurousness, in all likeliness they will initially resort to a reserved or even hesitant attitude. He might say to himself: let us just wait and see whether this change will work for or against me. He has noticed that time is wearing on faster than his mind can follow, and, above all, he has a feeling that this could mean the end of his routine too. Nothing will stay exactly as it was, all the constants in his day-to-day routine seem to have disappeared. This general sense of excitement surrounding this new era bothers him, and he cannot escape it.

So, I would urge you to abandon the perspective of the "doer" for a second and try to get a feel for the fears of your employees. When you tell your team excitedly about the concept of a paperless company, a cloud-based system, a social intranet, and a new business concept—which will open the work of each individual up to general criticism and further development—you will generate resistance. Employees actually value their ordered files, take pride in the storage organization of their hard drive, regard their data as confidential and could not care less about discussing every one of their work tasks. In a word: that person is uneasy and does not want to show it. They want to preserve tried and tested working approaches. After all, this is what brought them their long-standing reputation as a reliable employee in their company. This status is now at risk. They fear that someone else might fulfill these digital requirements better than they ever could or maybe even that a machine or a program might assume their role. These thoughts shake the foundations on which their livelihood is based. When the cracks start to form, they become distressed. From that point onward, their thoughts revolve around one fear: "I could lose my job."

Essentially, digitalization becomes the number one source of irritation in their life, and they themselves either turn into troublemakers or resign inwardly. Both outcomes would weaken the entire team.

That is why dialog is the first tool in the digital process. You will know how to quickly and flexibly apply your strategy to your department and to consolidate your information. You will identify the sources of mistakes and find solutions. You will improve efficiency by using programs. But what you must not forget is to talk, human-to-human. These should be the kind of talks where you close the door, switch off your phone, and ignore your e-mails. The kind where you look the other person in the eye, pay attention to their posture, word choice, and voice. The kind where you look for traces of concealed emotions and, as a result, in true manager style, opt for a gap analysis to obtain some benefit from the discussion.

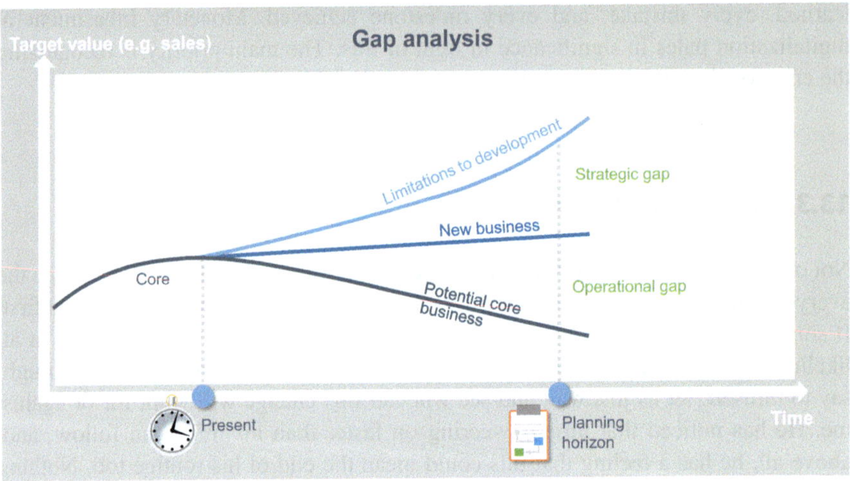


**Fig. 13.1** Gap analysis

A gap analysis (Fig. 13.1) is a management tool for depicting different assumptions of future business developments. Its aim is to identify gaps and concerns. The gap analysis centers around the following questions:

- Which future opportunities guarantee success?
- Which future risks will prevent success?

The mental horizon spans from the present into the planned future. This exploratory tool can give initial indications of potential gaps, but it is not intended as a replacement for strategy!

The gap analysis distinguishes between strategic and operational gaps. Strategic gaps—between the potential core business and the development limit—can be closed when new products are successfully developed after taking into account future potential. Operational gaps can be closed if all resources are used to optimize present core business (Gabler Wirtschaftslexikon 2017).

The gap analysis can be a means of identifying emotional gaps. A prevalence of fear and doubt leaves no room for enthusiasm. Fill these gaps with optimism. Take the edge off these fears by making clear to your employee how crucial his role is to success. Ask him to express his doubts, tell him not a word of it will leave this room and that it will be regarded as confidential. You will be surprised at what your employee reveals to you. Once they have voiced their fears, it is amazing how much more optimistic an employee can become, even rediscovering their creativity in many instances. It is as if all of the floodgates, once clogged up with doubt, have all been opened. According to the "Bitkom Digital Office Index 2016," those are the fears that digitalization could wipe out jobs, that they might not have the required expertise, that legal requirements and rights could change, that data could be lost, and that the paperless office could become a place without substance. "The survey shows that digitized processes are no longer a vision of the future—we are already on the way towards the digital workplace" (Biffar 2016).

But employees may hesitate en route too! Work out a plan together—before your employee stumbles and can no longer follow you. The gap analysis offers a question to assist with this: "Which conditions would you require to enable you to provide an optimum service?" Your employee might look back longingly to a time when he could still take an analog approach to his work. Grant him that. Let him delve into nostalgia before moving on to the following questions: "What, in your opinion, would be the ideal way to successfully position the company on the market? How would you proceed if there were no rules, no strategy and past either? What would be your future vision for our company?" These questions diffuse annoyance at present developments because the employee is involved from the outset. No amount of history can set a mission in stone. Everything can be approached from a new angle, and often this step back can be helpful. Then the employee suddenly comes to the realization that the company in which he has worked for a number of years has no option other than to initiate change. He realizes that the physical assets in which the company is investing are not putting jobs at risk, but providing more time and room for other tasks to put extra pressure on the competition. This realization is of fundamental importance. It shows the employee that digitalization will not put his job at risk, but that failure to initiate digitalization will.

Digitalization requires a changed way of thinking, and this applies to each individual employee. Insightful, empathic dialog can tear down any barriers. This is followed by a continuous training process. Remember my team sport analogy—a coach without a team would be pointless.

## 13.4 Team Mind Mapping

Management 4.0 could also be referred to as team 4.0 given that the questions raised by the change are a community issue. They dictate the daily work process. Learning from one another is the motto. A task may, for example, be: "We want to process our orders 100% digitally. What do we do to achieve that? How can we develop a trial phase? How much time do we need to implement it?" You can assume that the staff from order processing will provide you with the vital information, since it is they who deal with the issue on a day-to-day basis. The team thinks, and the manager pools these thoughts into a strategic line. One ideal approach to this would be mind mapping. This almost forgotten creative tool triggers the imagination while taking into account the experience of individuals. Despite its unfortunate mutation into a one-man mind game in days gone by, it has the potential to become an effective management 4.0 tool. Team mind mapping adds effortlessness to a process whose end result is a valuable contribution to digital strategy. Digital mind mapping programs turn results into graphics and use filters to spell out these results. They mirror thoughts using 3D technology:

- In your team, you draw or write associations on a screen.
- You accumulate common terms, issues, and experiences specific to the task at hand.
- You pool the results and provide them with headings.
- You decide the order and time period in which the individual steps are to be carried out.
- You regard the shared mind map as a binding working basis.

## 13.5 Digitalization Roadmap

Despite having stressed the exclusive importance of customer benefit to corporate success on multiple occasions in the preceding chapters, I would like to take this opportunity to again stress another key factor. The more your staff contribute to your digital strategy and embrace it with positive emotion, the more likely you are to be able to protect yourself against disruption by others. You remain attentive. You act with farsightedness. You retain your creativity. That is why—having reached the end of my book—I urge you again: do you not start without your staff. Draft a roadmap that you will return to, as a team, on a six monthly basis. The questions will remain the same, but the answers will change. That is because your neural network is learning because it is permanently responding to challenges with more creativity and less effort. Eventually you will reach the premier league, after having continually trained your adaptability and becoming a true master.

**Focus: Your Digital Agenda**

The following questions can be used as an aid for you and your team when drafting your digital agenda:

1. What ideas do we have for digitizing the working steps?
2. What technology and what programs do we need?
3. What timeline is appropriate, and what milestones should we set?
4. How can we become better than we are now?
5. Where can we learn, and what mistakes are we likely to make?
6. When will we get the sense that we are on the right path?
7. What fears are there, where do our assumptions about success deviate?
8. Are the milestones set out still appropriate, or do these need to be adapted?
9. Where is change forcing us to move faster?
10. Where are practical interfaces with upstream and downstream value chain stages emerging?
11. When can we interpret the demands of end customers?
12. Where are there hidden end customer hints, and how can we decide their nonverbal messages?

(continued)

13. Are all participants in the value chain smart enough to identify whether the benefit is changing, the product is changing, or the value chain is under disruptive attack?

The answers to these 13 questions indicate, on the one hand, how you are positioned in the value chain with your service and your vision. These can also show you where the weakest link in the chain (Fig. 13.2) is. This is where the risk of disruption is greatest. You should be attentive and actually ask yourselves as a team whether you can go along with these identified weaknesses or whether you yourself can take disruptive action and eliminate this weak link from the chain.

An overall analysis of digitized value chains illustrates the prerequisites for smooth operation: all stages must be linked up with one another—and communicate, in order to achieve optimum benefit at the end of the value chain. Digitized value chains are only as strong as their weakest link, if one link collapses, the entire chain is at risk. The basic prerequisite for success is a permanent consideration of the ultimate consumer benefit. This must be known to all and taken into account by all.

No one remains untouched by the digital revolution, not even managers. They are the ones who impart expertise with creativity and emotion. They radiate optimism by illustrating the humanity behind data. We cannot yet fully describe the ultimate meaning of management 4.0.

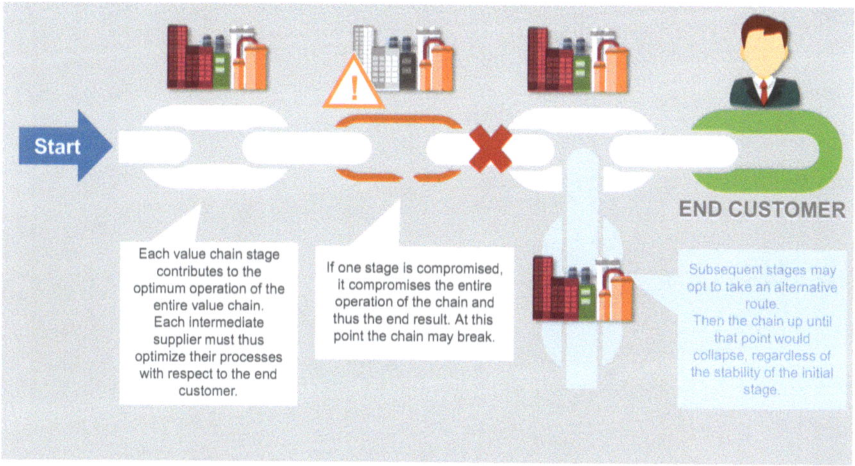


**Fig. 13.2** Risk of disruption

## References

Biffar J (2016) Press conference speech 'Bitkom Digital Office Index 2016'. https://www.bitkom.org/Presse/Anhaenge-an-PIs/2016/Maerz/Bitkom-Vortrag-Pressekonferenz-CeBIT-ECM-DOI-15-03-2016.pdf. Accessed 9 Feb 2017

Jobs S (2011). https://www.nzz.ch/sucht-was-euch-am-herzen-liegt-1.12903784. Accessed 9 Feb 2017

Maushagen P, Severin T (2016) Merkel will beim Datenschutz die Zügel lockern. http://de.reuters.com/article/deutschland-merkel-datenschutz-idDEKBN13C208. Accessed 9 Feb 2017

Springer Gabler Verlag (publisher) Gabler *Wirtschaftslexikon*, Stichwort: Gap-Analyse. http://wirtschaftslexikon.gabler.de/Archiv/85843/gap-analyse-v5. Accessed 9 Feb 2017

MIX
Papier aus verantwortungsvollen Quellen
Paper from responsible sources
FSC® C105338

If you have any concerns about our products,
you can contact us on
**ProductSafety@springernature.com**

In case Publisher is established outside the EU,
the EU authorized representative is:
**Springer Nature Customer Service Center GmbH**
**Europaplatz 3, 69115 Heidelberg, Germany**

Printed by Libri Plureos GmbH
in Hamburg, Germany